THREADS IN THE TAPESTRY

A Classical Christian Study of Genesis 1-11

Rev. Donald R. Sackett, M.Div.

PREFACE

Fr. Don Sackett is a gifted teacher and student of the Bible. He offers valuable insights to both the text and meaning of the opening chapters of the Book of Genesis. Some of our favorite Sunday School stories from Genesis Chapters 1-11 come to life as Fr. Sackett looks at what God is truly trying to share with us. The book is a good tool for teachers, preachers, or anyone simply looking to understand the Bible in their own personal devotion.

THE RT. REV. RYAN S. REED, SSC, D.D.

BISHOP OF FORT WORTH

ANGLICAN CHURCH IN NORTH AMERICA

Here is an evangelical plea and fervent study. The author has a pastor's heart and makes a humble offering for enlightenment; as well as an informed survey of the Church Catholic! This understanding of the Christian faith is historical and factual, and comes into a lost and bewildered secular society. Into this aimless world, God reveals Himself, and so a new world is in the making…!

The book traces the foundational biblical basis of the establishment of the new world order of Christian orthodoxy under the authority of the Vincentian Canon: that is to say, what has been (everywhere, always, and by all) is a threefold test of universality, antiquity, and consent! Hence, threefold orthodoxy… Catholic faith and order!

This book alone, with the Holy Spirit, will have blessed the reader Mightily! I commend this study of Brother Sackett's for your personal enrichment.

THE RT. REV. DR. LARRY SHAVER

CONTENTS

INTRODUCTION

When studying Genesis, it is important to understand that it answers some of the basic questions of humanity. Is there a god? Where did the universe come from? What is man? How did we get here? What is our purpose? What happens after death? Does this life matter?

Genesis, and for that matter the whole of Scripture, is a view of mankind from the eyes of our Creator. It is His perspective, a theological anthropology on who we are and why we are here. We aren't provided every detail of the creation of the world. We are only given the details that matter, yet the poetic nature of biblical Hebraic literature implies much more. You will see that through its literary structure, information is readily given that can only be understood by paying close attention to its repetitive structure. It is foundational writing that can satisfy our deepest questions.

Structure Of Genesis

On the basis of *content,* Genesis is divided into two sections: chapters 1:1-11:26 and chapters 11:27-50:26. **Genesis chapters 1-11** present an introduction to salvation history, describing the origin of the universe, the world, humanity, and sin. **Genesis 12-50** sets forth the origins of redemptive history through the patriarchs, the covenantal promised land, and posterity.

Moses is the author/scribe recording the message as dictated directly from God (Exodus 33:7-11; Numbers 12:8; John 5:45-47).

In the study of Scripture, it is wise to always follow the **Vincen-**

tian Canon:

> "The test of religious orthodoxy laid down by Vincent of Lerins, a monk of Lerins, Gaul, in the fifth century. In his commonitorium he states that what was Catholic was quod ubique, quod semper, quod ab omnibus creditum est (What has been believed everywhere, always, and by all), a three-fold test of universality, antiquity, and consent. He held that in relation to Scripture, the role of tradition was chiefly a guide to interpretation."[1]

The following are quotes from some of the Church Fathers concerning the authorship of Moses:

> "Notice this remarkable author, dearly beloved, and the particular gift he had. I mean, while all the other inspired authors told either what would happen after a long time or what was going to take place immediately, this blessed author, being born many generations after the event was guided by the deity on high and judged worthy to narrate what had been created by the Lord of all from the very beginning. Accordingly, he began with these words: "In the beginning God created heaven and earth." He well nigh bellows at us all and says, "Is it by human beings I am taught in uttering these things? It is the one who brought being from nothing who stirred my tongue in narrating them." Since we therefore listen to these words not as words of Moses but as the words of the God of all things coming to us through the tongue of Moses, so I beg you, let us heed what is said as distinguished from our own reasoning."[2] *– St. Chrysostom*

> "We are proposing to examine the structure of the world and to contemplate the whole universe, not from the wisdom of the world but from what God taught his servant when He spoke to him in person and without riddles."[3] *– St. Basil*

"What is the beginning of all things except our Lord and 'Savior of all,' Jesus Christ 'the firstborn of every creature?' In this beginning, therefore, that is, in His Word, 'God made heaven and earth' as the evangelist John also says in the beginning was the Word, and the Word was with God, and the Word was God. All things were made by Him, and without Him nothing was made."[4] – *Origen*

I pray, dear reader, that this work will challenge your faith and inspire your study of scripture.

CHAPTER 1

The first chapter of Genesis begins with the Name of God. "In the beginning God (*Elohim*) created the heavens and the earth." In Genesis God is revealed as "*Elohim*, which bespeaks, [1] The power of God the Creator. *El* signifies the strong God; and what less than almighty strength could bring all things out of nothing? [2] The plurality of the persons of the Godhead, Father, Son, and Holy Ghost. This plural name of God, in Hebrew, which speaks of him as many though he is one, confirming our faith in the doctrine of the Trinity, which, though but darkly intimated in the Old Testament, is clearly revealed in the New. We are often told that the world was made by him, and nothing made without him (John 1:3 10; Ephesians 3:9; Colossians 1:16; Hebrews 1:2)."[5] The Name establishes God as the exclusive creator. There is nothing above or before Him, therefore, He is prime reality. The first verse of Genesis establishes that before anything in the material universe existed, God existed. His existence precedes the material universe and also undergirds the Church's teaching that nothing material pre-existed. All that exists was made from nothing, *ex-nihilo*. The "beginning" refers to both the material universe as well as the commencement of time.

Instead of looking at the cosmos as chaos, Genesis one describes the earth as a blank canvas – not chaos. *St. Ambrose* taught "Scripture points out that things were first created and afterward put in order."[6] But not everything at that time existed which we shall see as the narrative progresses. The earth was unformed, in that it existed but was shapeless. It was there, but covered in water. There was darkness, and The Spirit of God fluttered, brooding, hovering, over the face of the waters.

The Creation Of Time

"And God said . . ." how many times does this phrase occur in the first chapter? This is the beginning of something important. Moses uses a Hebrew poetic literary style of repetition, which serves to draw our attention to important details, because there is a wealth of information contained therein. For example, the repeated phrase, *"and God said,"* is like a flashing arrow that points to the fact that creation is accomplished by the Word of God.

God's first command had to do with light. The light wasn't just any light. *"Let there be light."* Where did this light come from? God didn't create the sun and moon until the 4th day, so where does it come from? Revelation 21:22-24 gives us a hint in its description of the heavenly city. Verse 23 says, *"and the city had no need of the sun, neither of the moon, to shine in it: for the glory of God did lighten it, and the Lamb is the light thereof."* The light comes from the second person of the Trinity, Jesus Christ (John 1:1-5). This light is a divine light. This is why God said "it is good." The divine light is preferred over darkness. So at the beginning of creation, the universe was lit by divine light, and so it will be again throughout all eternity after Christ returns.

What is a day in scripture? St. Peter wrote in his epistle *"that one day is with the Lord as a thousand years, and a thousand years as one day."* Does that mean that the *"day"* described in Genesis is also *"as a thousand years?"* Verse five of chapter one explains: *"And God called the light Day, and the darkness he called Night. And the evening and the morning were the first day."* The purpose of the light was to divide, and God called the light day and the darkness night.

Notice there is no riddle in this passage of scripture. It is very literal and descriptive. We are given a measurement of time: one day. In Genesis chapter one, a day is from sunrise to sunset. There is no illusion to 1,000 years at all. This is a very literal measurement, and again Moses repeated this statement to draw attention to this important detail. *"There was evening and there was morning"* reinforces the measurement of time, and also demonstrates to us that the creation of time does not deviate. A day is from sunrise to sunset, a week is seven days, there is a consistency, it does not change.

There is also a clear structure in the process of creation. "Each command consists of (1) an announcement, *"God said;"* (2) a creative command, *"Let there be"*; (3) a summary word of accomplishment, *"And it was so"*; (4) a descriptive word of accomplishment, *"The earth brought forth"*; (5) a descriptive blessing, *"God Blessed"*; (6) an evaluative approval, *"it was good"*; and (7) a concluding temporal framework, numbering each day."[7] The structure, and repetition of that structure, show us how God created with His Word, and demonstrates to us that whatever God commands will be accomplished. There was nothing left undone. It shows us that we can trust that God's word will be fulfilled, always, just as it was at the beginning of creation.

On each day in the process of creation, everything He created was blessed. Each portion was evaluated and approved by God, showing that each part of creation was good. This is also a very important theme of scripture. He, being spirit, creates matter and approves it. *"The earth brought forth"* shows us that all matter obeyed his Word. God was not bound by the laws of physics. He created them, and they serve Him.

According To Its Kind

The next repetition we see is that each creature, the birds of the air, things under the sea, and the creatures on dry land were all created *"according to its kind."* This assertion is not only found in the creation narrative, but it is repeated throughout the Pentatuch[8] in reference to the things created by God. The repetition of *"according to its kind"*, especially in the creation account, emphasizes that God created everything very specifically. There was no randomness to His creation, and we see evidence of this in creation today. Creatures still replicate themselves after their own kind, and there is no real evidence to the contrary.

What is known as macro-evolution — the idea that one creature, given enough time, can evolve into another *kind* of creature — is a theory that has yet to be proven by any real evidence. However, evidence of microevolution — small developments that happen over time within a particular species — is well established.

Even all plant life was created *"according to its kind"* and still replicates that process today. Every plant and creature on earth was specifically and purposefully created by God, including you. This is a foundational understanding of the world. Everything was created with intention and order, by an intentional and orderly being, according to an overarching plan. This understanding gives us peace of mind and an understanding of the world around us. When we begin to question the truth of this foundational message, we create confusion and fear that, over time, can have disastrous effects on our view of the world and our culture.

The Creation Of Man

On the sixth day of creation God said, *"Let us make Man in our own likeness."*

"There is here this deliberation, collaboration and communion not because God needs advice – God forbid saying such a thing! But so that the very impact of the language of our creation would show us honor."[9] – *St. Chrysostom*

Here we see that there is a plurality to God. It is our first exposure to the Trinity. God deliberates within the godhead saying *"let us"* which indicates both a unity of persons but also a plurality.

Regarding the creation of man, Gregory of Nyssa said,

"This same language was not used for (the creation) of other things. The command was simple when light was created; God said, "Let there be light." Heaven was also made without deliberation... These, though, were before (the creation of) humans. For humans, there was deliberation. He did not say, as he did when creating other things, "Let there be a human." See how worthy you are! Your origins are not an imperative. Instead, God deliberated about the best way to bring life to a creation worthy of honor."[10]

Likeness Of God

The theme of *"after their kind"* is important in the creation of man, also. God, who is the creator, is transcendent. He is not of heaven and earth, but, creator of heaven and earth. In the creation of man, God established a creature that is after His own kind, so he created man in his likeness. Up until this point, God created things according to their own likeness. The grass was created according to its own likeness. The birds, the things in the sea, the creatures on land, they are all created *"after their kind."* But man is made according to the likeness of God. He is not made according to what is found in heaven and earth, but rather according to the creator, according to God's likeness. He is not God, yet he is made in the likeness of God.

The process of creation was intimate and purposeful. Everything was made so that life could be sustained. As God concluded his creation, he surveyed all of creation and pronounced it to be *"very good."* This approval, pronounced by the creator, shows that nothing was incomplete. Everything that existed was created in its fullness and completeness, including mankind.

Have you ever worked on a creative project and felt there was something missing? There's unrest, a pressing drive to continue the work until it is right, until it is complete, until it is perfect. The pronouncement of *"it was very good"* shows us that nothing was left undone or incomplete. His work was complete and he was pleased. Then, on the seventh day, God rested.

CHAPTER 2

A Closer Look At Man

The first chapter of Genesis is an overall summary of the work of creation. It establishes some very specific principles. As we move on to chapter two, we will follow these same principles as we look more closely at the creation of man. Chapter two is not a separate, second version of creation but rather a different perspective: a closer look at God's work in creating mankind.

The conclusion of the creation narrative is found at the beginning of chapter two. Chapter breaks and verses were added to the text well after their writing as a means of reference points. The original texts did not include them. The first chapter encapsulates the first six days of creation. In chapter two, the seventh day is described, and then the text moves into a more in-depth explanation of the creation of man.

At this point, we've already met the Almighty God, who speaks of himself in the plural, and yet there is a unity that cannot be ignored. In Genesis 1:2 we are shown the Holy Spirit, who hovers over all creation. We also see that there is a light that divides the darkness, which is the preincarnate Son of God, Jesus Christ. Our Triune God is uncreated and pre-existent, working to create all things. You will not find the term "Holy Trinity" in any scriptural text, yet that concept is abundantly clear throughout.

John 1:1-5 gives another version of creation, and begins with the same phrase *"In the beginning."*

There are three points to examine in Genesis chapter two. First, God rested from His work on the seventh day. Next, a River went out from Eden. Finally, we'll explore the creation of man, animals, women, and the consequences of man's actions.

In verse one, God surveys all that he created and declares all of it finished and complete. God's work is so intentional that it's repeated poetically in verse two. *"And on the seventh day God ended His work which He had made; and He rested on the seventh day from all His work which He had made."* (Genesis 2:2) There are several assertions in these statements. The first is the clear reinforcement that there was no other way the earth was created. God made the earth, using his rational intelligence and divine will.

Work And Rest

These verses also show us that work is good because God both performs work and commands it. This message is also discussed in 2 Thessalonians 3:10 when the Apostle Paul says that if a man does not work, neither should he eat. The value of work is even carried further, as we see that work is completed in the daytime, and balanced out by rest in the evening. Rest is another important concept illustrated in these verses. As God rested on the seventh day, so should man, for we are made in His likeness.

Verse three says God blessed the seventh day and sanctified it. This is significant because it demonstrates that we need to take time to focus upon the sacred. It is also an allegory of the eternal rest that is to come for all believers, another demonstration that matter (created things) is sacred, though matter can be corrupted.

A Closer Look At The Creation Of Man

Chapter one was written in a literary style that makes it easy to remember and employs literary devices to aid memorization providing emphasis on certain points. This continues in chapter two as we see the creation of man. The text emphasizes that man was created out of virgin clay and called Adam. Adam was formed of the dust of [the adama] *virgin earth* verses 4-6, God breathed into his nostrils the breath of life; and man became a living soul. Virgin clay was used to form the earth-man; earth was mixed with the breath of God. (Overwhelming complexity)

Why does it matter that God formed man from virgin clay? Why did God use clay? Red virgin clay is pliable, moist, and unblemished. At this point, the earth was complete, pure, and uncorrupted. There were no decomposing elements mixed into the earth. God scooped the pure clay out of the earth and formed it into man. Then he breathed into the clay the breath of life and man became a living soul. Can you picture this loving, intimate act? Imagine God patiently, carefully sculpting the first man in his own image and then gently leaning over His creation, breathing the life of the Holy Spirit into him. What a beautiful demonstration of God's care and love for each of us. A simple description to describe something overwhelmingly complex.

Garden Of Eden And The Temple Of God

Eden is a type and shadow of the Church, allegorically speaking. It is the perfect habitat for man and is the most full and fruitful place on earth. From it flows the great rivers of the earth. It's filled with trees that provide food for man. It is the center of creation and the cradle of life. Within it also stands the tree of the knowledge of good and evil, as well as the tree of life.

Eden also contains gold and precious stones, the very stones found on the breastplate of Aaron the High Priest of God to Israel[11]. These same stones are used in the construction of the Celestial City of God that comes down out of heaven in Revelation 21:18-21, *"The construction of its wall was of jasper; the city was pure gold, like clear glass. The foundations of the wall of the city were adorned with all kinds of precious stones: the first foundation was jasper, the second sapphire, the third chalcedony, the fourth emerald, the fifth sardonyx, the sixth sardus, the seventh chyrolite, the eighth beryl, the ninth topaz, the tenth chrysoprase, the eleventh jacinth, the twelfth amethyst. The gates were twelve pearls: each individual gate was one pearl. And the street of the city was pure gold, like transparent glass."*

The weather is pleasant and there is no precipitation, for the earth is watered from underground springs. Trees provide food, wisdom, and life, prefiguring the Cross of Christ in the midst of the Church which provides the same nourishment.

The Garden prefigures the Temple of God, a copy of the true temple in heaven, and Adam is its priest. Adam is placed in the temple as God's representative, he is the image bearer of God, to sanctify its fruit and offer it in worship to God. The early church fathers had much to say about this.

St. Cyprian said, "The Church, expressing the image of paradise, encloses fruitful trees within its walls. From these whatever does not make good fruit is cut off and cast into the fire."[12]

St. Jerome commented, "Now if wisdom is the tree of life, Wisdom itself indeed is Christ. You understand now that the man who is blessed and holy is compared to this tree – that is, he is compared to Wisdom. Consequently, you see too that the just man, that blessed man who has not followed the council of the wicked – who has not done that but has done this – is like the tree that is planted near running water. He is, in other words, like Christ, in as much as he "raised us up together and seated us together in heaven."[13]

St. Basil the Great wrote, "For this reason we look to the east in our prayers, but few know that this is because we are seeking the ancient fatherland, which God planted in Eden, toward the east."[14]

Man Is Given Work

In verse 15, the Lord God took the man he had formed and put him in the garden to tend it. Man is given a role and responsibility. His role is to tend and keep the garden, yet he is more than a gardener. Adam is made in the image of God and is singular in his kind besides God. Adam is made of matter and all matter is good. So Adam presides in the highest place and governs as high priest over all creation. In giving Adam work, he also gave him freedom.

"The meaning of freedom is defined in the creation narratives. In Genesis 1:28 it is implied that we are created to make real choices between real options, even though this freedom is bound by the prescription to be fruitful and rule the earth. Without the freedom to make real choices it would be impossible to rule. In recognition of this, most English versions of the Bible translate Genesis 2:16 as permission to "freely eat" of all the trees in the garden. There is no "freely" in the Hebrew text which, in fact, uses the same construction here that is used in verse 17, *you will surely die.*" In this context we see that Adam and Eve have the freedom to choose what to eat from all the trees, but they have no freedom as to the consequences if they eat of the one forbidden tree. Thus with freedom and responsibility comes a test of obedience in the prohibition placed on eating from the tree of the knowledge of good and evil." [15]

This freedom shows us the mental faculties with which Adam was created. He is innocent in virtue and character, he possesses the capacity to receive instruction, make free-will choices, and to make practical and moral decisions. In chapter two, Adam demonstrates creative and administrative skills in naming the animals. He used critical thinking and other executive skills. Adam also recognized that there was none other of his "kind" and realized that he was alone. He was self-aware. He also had an understanding of the complex and abstract. Death had not yet entered the world, and yet he understood what death was when God mentions it in vs. 17. Chapter two shows us that Adam was created with full intellectual faculties.

This brings us to Adam's God given assignment to tend ('abad) and keep (shamar) the garden. A better translation would read, *"to serve"* and *"to guard."* In Numbers 3:7-8 and 8:26 the Lord gives the Levites the authority to minister in the tabernacle. It is no coincidence that the same Hebrew words are given in the same order to convey the priestly role to which Aaron and his sons were called.

There are additional parallels that help us understand that Adam is the high priest of humanity. As Aaron was clothed at God's command, so too Adam is clothed with garments by God (Genesis 3:21; Exodus 28:42; Deuteronomy 23:13-14). The high priests' garments were arrayed with gold and onyx; so too is there mention of gold and onyx in Eden (Genesis 2:11-12; Exodus 25:7). As Aaron cannot draw near to God with his nakedness exposed, so too after the fall, Adam cannot draw near to God with his nakedness exposed (Genesis 3:10; Exodus 20:26, 28:42).

Adam was to fulfill the duties of a priest, which are to minister in the sanctuary and do what all priests do: offer sacrifice. He must guard (shamar) the garden; this implies that there must be something to guard it from. This leads us to the question of what Adam is called to sacrifice.

"When the serpent enters the garden, i.e. the sanctuary, we have a good idea of what he is supposed to be guarding against, namely Satan, sin and death. Now, most of all, he is to attend to his priestly duties. The "gifts and sacrifices" Adam is called to offer is none other than the gift and sacrifice of his very self, for his bride, so as to save her from Satan, sin and death. This is made most clear when we consider what Jesus, the new Adam, did (cf. 1 Corinthians 15:45). He offered the gift and sacrifice of himself for his bride, the church, so as to save her from Satan, sin and death. Unfortunately, Adam stands by silently as his bride deals with the life-threatening serpent, and we have been affected by the consequences ever since."[16]

Because of Adam's failure we are introduced to the idea that disobedience to God's Word brings death. Verses 16-17 are not simply a prohibition against *"touching"* the fruit. This passage shows how God gave man free will, and also demonstrates man's ability to reason and make choices. Up until this point, God's word is creative, and all matter obeys His Word. In this verse, we learn that disobedience to God's word brings death into the world. Adam's disobedience would betray his Divine directive to *"keep"* and thus cuts him off from the tree of life and therefore eternal life.

Here we will see in Eden a type and shadow of the church. Contained within it, at the center, is the tree of life, which is a type and shadow of the crucifix. Sin expels us from the church and eternal life by separating us from the Cross. More on that later.

There is no prohibition in God's original instruction about *"touching"* the fruit. Instead he specifically said, *"you will not eat of it."* Later, in chapter three, we'll see an additional boundary created by man not to *"touch"* the fruit. This gives us a glimpse into Adam's character.

The Creation Of Woman

God said it is *"not good"* for man to be alone. All of creation is complete, but it is not complete without the creation of woman. This is the only thing thus far described in this way. Once Eve is formed, only then is creation declared *"VERY GOOD."* God's plan would not be complete without women. Woman is not an afterthought.

God wanted Adam to realize his loneliness. God paraded in front of Adam a male and female of every beast for him to name, but nothing that was compatible for Adam.

Woman came from Adam, earthman, endowed with a soul (the breath of life). God caused Adam to sleep and took a rib from Adam to form a woman. Woman means "from man." God makes the first woman from man, and yet for the rest of time, man comes forth from woman. Man cannot procreate without woman, and woman cannot procreate without man.

The First Society

Chapter two of Genesis provides important clues regarding man's relationship with God, with woman, and with creation. Woman was called Adam's *"help meet."*

"Help" is a word frequently used in the Psalms. It is not a degrading position for the woman. The verb form basically means to aid or supply that which the individual cannot provide for himself. The Septuagint[17] translates it *boethos,* a word the New Testament uses in the sense of "physician" (Matt 15:25; Mark 9:22,24; Acts 16:9; Rev 12:16). It conveys the idea of aiding someone in need, such as the oppressed. "Certainly a godly woman meets this need of man. *'Meet'* comes from the Hebrew word meaning 'opposite.' Literally it is 'according to the opposite of him,' meaning that she will complement and correspond to him. The Septuagint has *kat' auton* (according to him). This relates to a 'norm' or 'standard.' She is to be equal to and adequate for man. Not on the animal level of being."[18]

This relationship between God, Adam and Eve is the cornerstone of the first society. We also see the first marriage. The great historian Flavius Josephus understood this passage to indicate that the first thing Adam did when he saw her was to make love to her immediately. From a biblical perspective, this brought about both a physical and spiritual bond between Adam and the woman. He declared her *"bone of my bone, flesh of my flesh."* This union establishes a society based in marriage between one man and one woman. Adam's naming of Woman shows his continued role of stewardship, not in the sense of ownership, but headship and responsibility.

The Apostle Paul wrote in I Corinthians 11, *"But I would have you know that the head of every man is Christ, and the head of the woman is the man, and the head of Christ is God."* Paul was explaining the God given constructs of the ideal society, and also what was established in Genesis chapter two. Man now has a counterpart that was created for him, to compliment him. There is no domination expressed in this relationship, but rather a loving and mutual submission to one another. That is why God declared it to be *"very good."* Oppression is when either a man or a woman behaves in a way outside this relationship that was ordained by God.

Finally we learn that Adam and Eve are naked at creation, which is an indication of their moral innocence and purity. The pureness of the soul was seen through the flesh of Adam and Eve. This pureness was light, which shone through the flesh concealing the unseemly parts of the body.[19] As we will see, sin defiled mankind concealing the soul behind what became mortal flesh, as opposed to an immortal glorified body, in turn revealing the unseemly portions of the flesh. All creation is now complete. Adam and Eve lack nothing. They have perfect communion with nature, with each other, and with God. This glorified form is what mankind will be returned to at the Resurrection.[20]

CHAPTER 3

The Fall Of Mankind

Have you ever eaten nuts from their shell? It's a lot of work, cracking the nut and picking the meat from the shell. But never does a nut taste so sweet as when it's picked fresh from the shell. It's been said that the Old Testament is like a nut with a very hard shell. You must break through the outer shell in order to enjoy the sweet meat within. The New Testament is described as the sweet meat. Without the shell, the meat of the nut spoils and sickens the belly. The tough outer shell preserves the rich goodness of its treasure, but it must be cracked and opened in order to discover the sweet meat.

That's what we're doing in this study. We're cracking open the nut to reveal the sweet meat of the gospel.

Graeme Goldsworthy wrote, "There are certain elements of New Testament teaching which we see the person and work of Jesus Christ as answering the temptation and fall of mankind as recorded in Genesis three. In those terms, the gospel makes sense only if there was a real temptation and fall which radically altered the course of human nature and the history of mankind thereafter. We must assert that there really was one man, Adam, through whom sin and death entered the world, as St. Paul says in Romans 5:12."[21]

There are three parts to the account of the Fall of Man: The Temptation, The Fall, and The Curse. We'll look at each part carefully.

The Temptation

Verse one of chapter three tells us the serpent was more subtle (*cunning*) than all creatures. 1 Chronicles 21:1; 2 Corinthians 11:3-4; and Job 1:6 shows us how the serpent is a type and shadow of Satan. Through this creature God shows us exactly how Satan works. He manipulates language to cause us to question God's Word and its authority. History has proven that whoever controls the language controls the narrative. This passage introduces us to that concept through the serpent's subtle questioning.

Through this dialogue, the serpent shows that he had been watching and waiting, looking for an opportunity to tempt the humans. It's clear that the serpent knows and understands God's command, and he also understands the relationship between Adam and Eve. It's interesting that he chooses to challenge Adam indirectly through Eve. The serpent begins by agreeably miss-representing God's command. Eve is engaged to provide motherly correction to the serpent saying *"nor shall you touch it, lest you die."* God said, "<u>lest</u> ye die." In verse 2:16-17 Eve said, "Thou shalt <u>*surely*</u> die."

Here the serpent switches tactics and begins to contradict God's word. *"You shall not die by death."* This play on words implies that God's word is false. *"For God knows that when you eat of it you shall be like gods."* God's command protected Adam and Eve from the loss of eternal life. The serpent instead applies the language to mortal life. This subtle misdirection challenges the truth and authority of God's Word. How is this done today in our postmodern culture?

There's also an implication that God is keeping things from Adam and Eve that would make them complete. Can God be trusted? The serpent implies that he can't, and cunningly suggests that man's reason should be the higher authority, rather than God's word. "Both God and His Word are seen as lesser authorities that must constantly be tested by higher authorities. Again the cunning of the snake: he does not suggest that humans transfer their allegiance from God to himself, but only that they themselves should consider and evaluate God's claim to truth."[22] "Do thine own will." This same tactic is used in the temptation of Christ in Matt 4:4; 4:7; 4:10. We too are tempted in the same subtle ways. This dialogue is a blueprint for how Satan works to tempt us to sin by questioning the truth of God's word.

The Fall

Then Adam said, *"It was the woman"* who took the fruit *"desired to make one wise, she took . . . and did eat, and gave also to her husband with her; and he did eat."* The first lesson for us in this passage is what happens when communion with God is broken. In that moment, sin and shame entered the world. God came looking for Adam and Eve, and they hid themselves from him. Who among us hasn't done the same thing? We skip church, avoid prayer, and fill our lives with distractions to avoid God and His healing presence. Just like Adam and Eve, it is our sin that separates us from God and fills us with shame.

Adam and Eve, in eating the fruit, rejected the word of God in an effort to be like God. St. Paul references this original sin in Romans chapter one, beginning at verse 18, *"Because that which may be known of God is manifest in them; for God hath shewed it unto them. For the invisible things of him from the creation of the world are clearly seen, being understood by the things that are made, even his eternal power and Godhead; so that they are without excuse."* They desired to be in the place of God. They were convinced that by taking the fruit, they wouldn't need God any longer.

After the fruit is eaten, we see evidence that there was a mental and emotional change in Adam and Eve. First, we're told *"their eyes were opened, and they became ashamed."* Before eating the fruit, they were *"naked and unashamed,"* they were innocent. This reveals a spiritual change and a loss of innocence. Their innocence allowed them to be at peace with God and with each other, and to live without fear. But now their disobedience caused them to fear, hide, and be filled with shame.

Adam and Eve heard the sound of the Lord God walking/traversing, *"the voice of the Lord God which was going through the garden on the wind/spirit of the day."* "Conceived anthropomorphically, God walks on the clouds (Ps 104:3) or in the heavens (Job 22:14). More frequently, and more importantly is applied to Yahweh's coming to his people in judgment or blessing (2 Sam 7:23; Ps 80:2)."[23] Adam and Eve hid themselves among the trees of the garden from the presence of the Lord God. *"By hiding they are acknowledging their broken fellowship with God."*[24]

The passage also shows lust entering the world and how the serpent created covetousness in the heart of the woman, which is the "lust of the eyes."[25] Beyond this, we see in chapter two verse five the serpent tells Eve, *"for God doth know that in the day ye eat thereof, then your eyes shall be opened, and ye shall be as gods, knowing good and evil."* The consequence of lust is always broken relationship. Any time we choose to obey our lust rather than God, we set ourselves up as a god, and that is never good.

A key word in this passage is *"knowing."* Knowing becomes a play on words. Later, in chapter four, we learn that Adam "knew" Eve, and she conceived a son. "Knowing" in this case, it means an intimate knowledge of good and evil, which is a loss of innocence. Though Adam and Eve lived as man and wife, they remained innocent until they took the fruit and became aware of their own nakedness. Lust is an inordinate desire to satisfy the flesh, which comes out of the idea that we are incomplete. The lie is that anything other than communion with God can complete us.

Adam, Eve, and the serpent are now all subject to God's judgment. The one who created everything good came looking for Adam and Eve and found them in a state of sin. God is the ultimate authority of all creation, therefore he judged them. The serpent received his due punishment, as did Adam and Eve.

The Curse

The Serpent is cursed for what he did. He must crawl on his belly eating dust. The entire animal kingdom is fallen and radically changed due to the fall. We will see this as we look at the details of the judgment God imposes for Adam and Eve's sin.

Protoevangelium - The First Gospel

In addition to the curse, which changes all of creation, we are also presented with the first Gospel (Genesis 3:15). This is also known as the *Protoevangelium*. Through the seed of woman, victory would be gained over the serpent. The *seed* of woman is Christ, and the serpent is Satan.

Woman, for her role in the fall, is told that God will *"Multiply thy sorrow in thy conception . . ."* Pain is now a reality in a fallen world. Furthermore, *"thy desire shall be to thy husband, and he shall rule over thee."* Here the word *"desire"* is full of meaning. It does not only mean a physical desire for man, but also a desire for his role as head of the family and of society. In some ways, the roots of modern feminism can be found in Eve.

"As soon as we abandon a secularistic interpretation of the Bible, we can perceive that, from a supernatural point of view, women are actually granted a privileged position in the economy of redemption. Those who persist in wearing secularisitic lenses have eyes and do not see, have ears and do not hear, for the Bible cannot be understood except in an attitude of humble receptivity, that is, "on one's knees," (as Kierkegaard puts it). So-called 'biblical scholars' may know Aramaic and Greek but nevertheless radically misunderstand the divine message, because their 'scholarship' has warped their faith. A tacit refusal to receive God's message – because of intellectual pride – is punished by blindness."[26]

Then God said to Adam, *"Because you listened to the voice of your wife, cursed is the ground because of you. By the sweat of your face you shall eat bread."* Hard labor! The earth is now corrupted due to sin. Weeds grow as a consequence. No longer will nature cooperate with man in the same way it did in the garden. "The freedom to eat from the trees is now replaced by the struggle to get food from the earth. The soil is no longer servant to Adam and Eve."[27]

After the curse, man named his wife Eve, calling her *"the mother of all living."* Clement of Alexandria comments, "The woman who initiated transgression was called "Life," because she was responsible for the succession of those who came to birth and sinned. She thus became mother of the righteous and unrighteous alike. Each one of us shows himself to be just or willfully renders himself disobedient." [28]

Then God covers man's nakedness with the skin of animals in verses 20-21. Here we see the first sacrifice for sin. A blood sacrifice is implied and also vicarious suffering for sin. In this case, Adam and Eve's sin required a life to be taken—a blood sacrifice, a sacrament. In a symbolic way, the animal took on the sin and suffered in their place. This is a prefiguring of the sacrificial worship of God.

From this point on, those who would worship God must bring forth a blood sacrifice (also called a "sin offering"), which opens communion with God. God is so righteous that he cannot abide sin, therefore a blood sacrifice is required to cover our sin in order for us to have communion with Him. Centuries later, in Leviticus, sacrificial worship became more regulated and illustrated the fullness of what Christ would accomplish in His Passion. This worship continued, virtually unchanged, until Christ's sacrifice on the cross. This is how it has been since Adam and Eve, and we see this same worship reflected in today's Catholic and Orthodox churches. Christ's once-for-all-time bloody sacrifice is remembered in the Mass, using the symbols of bread and wine.

The Communing Of God Within Himself

In verse 22, God once again communes within himself. *"Behold, man has become like one of us, knowing good and evil."* This communing shows us that Almighty God is triune. The use of plural pronouns reveals both a unity and a division within the personhood of God. This phrase also mocks the statement of the serpent, who told Eve that she would be like God when she ate the fruit. But in reality, their sin marred their likeness and separated them from God.

"And the Lord God said, Behold, the man is become as one of us, to know good and evil: and now, lest he put forth his hand, and take also of the tree of life, and eat, and live forever: Therefore the Lord God sent him forth from the garden of Eden, to till the ground from whence he was taken. So, He drove out the man; and He placed at the east of the garden of Eden Cherubims, and a flaming sword which turned every way, to keep the way of the tree of life."[29]

"The name [cherubim] means 'fullness of knowledge' or 'outpouring of wisdom.' This first of the hierarchies (including seraphim and cherubim) is hierarchically ordered by truly superior beings, for this hierarchy possesses the highest order as God's immediate neighbor, being grounded directly around God and receiving the primal theophanies and perfections. Hence the description is 'carrier of warmth' for the seraphim, and the title is 'outpouring of wisdom' for the cherubim. These names indicated their similarity to what God is... the name cherubim signifies the power to know and to see God, to receive the greatest gifts that bring wisdom and to share these generously with subordinates as a part of the beneficent outpouring of wisdom. – *Pseudo-Dionysius. Celestial Hierarchies 7.205B-205C.*[30]

"Eating the fruit did indeed mean that the humans came to know good and evil. But the process by which they achieved that involved a rebellion against truth and its source. Instead of knowing good and evil by rejecting evil and remaining good, they choose rather to reject good and become evil . . . They rebel against God not by consciously making Satan their new final authority, but by taking that function to themselves. The truth of any proposition would from this point onward be tested by what was in humans themselves. In this sense they *became as God.*"[31]

If this statement is true then it should be self-evident today as well. The temple setting of the garden was guarded by the Cherubim. When man sinned his sin was forgiven by God, but the consequences of sin remained. Eden stands as a type of the church and represents communion with God. Man's excommunication from the Garden is one of those consequences. Adam and Eve became separated from communion with God, lost their innocence, and caused death to enter the world.

CHAPTER 4

Adam And Eve Have Children

Chapter four begins outside the garden of Eden. The focus of chapter four is on the struggle of fallen man. Vanity and futility are now part of the human story. This chapter reveals a lifetime of information about Adam and Eve. But *time compression* is still in effect, so we are only presented with the information that is important for us to know. This is not an exhaustive history of the first couple, but rather a presentation of key points from their lives.

"Adam knew his wife." This is the first mention of marital intercourse in the Bible. Some see this as a first, but we must remember that Adam and Eve, before the fall were pronounced *"good,"* and commanded to *"be fruitful, and multiply, fill the earth, and subdue it."* We must be careful not to make marital intercourse a result of the fall.

Here we also find the beginning of the redemption story in the seed of Adam and Eve. The seed, which was first mentioned in chapter three, verse 15, is the Messianic line, the line of Christ. All of Biblical history follows the line of the seed, and will be the main focal point going forward.

The Birth Of Cain And Abel

Adam and Eve produced a child through God. It was with God's help that this happened. This acknowledges the importance of marriage. But more than that, in the future, many of the women who bear the messianic seed are barren until God intervenes. God's involvement in the process shows us that human life is not random. According to the biblical narrative, God is involved in the process of procreation. Eve acknowledges this when she says, *"I have gotten a man from the Lord"* in verse one.

"Knew" in verse one refers to the "knowledge" of sexual relations. It is also the connecting link to the whole creation narrative; note the appearance of the word in connection with the tree of knowledge in verses one, 17, and 25. Later in the story, the replacing of a son by "knowing" is antithetical to the murder, which is denied in verse nine by, "I know not." Some take "from the Lord" as an accusative: *"I have gotten a man, from the Lord."* But the preposition is better as, *"I have created, acquired a man with [the help of] Jehovah!"* Thus Eve sees her generative power as part of the sharing of the divine power: "Jehovah formed man; I have formed the second man."

Names mean everything. Cain in this case is significant. The name literally means "acquire." St. Augustine said, "Note that the name of Cain means 'ownership,' which explains what was said at the time of his birth by his father or mother: 'I have come into possession of a man through God.'"[32]

A Statement Of Faith

"It is obvious that Eve's utterance was the dictate of faith. In Cain's birth she recognized the earnest and guarantee of the promised seed, and in token of her faith gave her child a name which may also explain her use of the divine name Jehovah instead of Elohim, which she employed when conversing with the serpent."[33]

"That Eve denominates her infant a man has been thought to indicate that she had previously borne daughters who had grown to womanhood, and that she expected her young tender babe to reach maturity."[34]

While it's important that Eve recognizes God's hand in the creative process, she also has unrealistic expectations. Her statement demonstrates that she expects her firstborn to bring forth the messianic seed and put an end to man's toil through a prophesied redemptive work.

Adam and Eve's second son was Abel. Abel's name literally means *vapor, breath.* Figuratively, it means vanity. "The name suggests that Eve's hopes had already begun to be disappointed in her elder son, or that having in her first child's name expressed her faith, in this she desires to preserve a monument of the miseries of human life, of which, perhaps, she had been forcibly reminded by her own maternal sorrows. It is thought that Cain and Able were twins, though the text is not specific."[35]

Cain was a tiller of the ground, while Abel was a keeper of the sheep. Adam and Eve and their family are fallen and have been driven out of the garden, but God has not abandoned them. God is not aloof in this narrative. He is close and intimate. But clearly, there were rules about how to approach God. Beginning in verse three, the two men brought forth an offering for the Lord. This implies an organized and regulated worship, because there were acceptable and unacceptable sacrifices.

"Genesis four illustrates human sinfulness and what its logical outcome is in human relationships. Cain refuses God's verdict in which his offering is rejected and his brothers accepted. He responds with anger directed at Abel and kills him. Human conflict is thus shown to be the consequence of broken fellowship with God. There is anger at the grace of God when it is shown to another."[36]

Even though Abel gives his offering by faith (Heb. 11: 4), grace is still the reality at work here.

"Grace shown to Abel is representative of the kindness of God that will be shown to men and women down through the ages. It provokes Cain to anger and thus demonstrates its effect of bringing about an actual distinction between those who receive it and those who don't. This distinction is an essential and continuing part of revelation throughout the biblical story."[37]

Abel's offering was acceptable because it was a blood sacrifice and follows the example that was established by God. (Genesis 3:21). Thus, he acknowledged that his sin deserved death and could be covered only by the death of a guiltless sacrifice (Hebrews 9:22). That his lamb was a firstling and fat implies that he gave the best he had in contrast to Cain's offering. Abel's offering was more excellent (Hebrews 11:4) because it was the right kind of offering and was made with the right heart attitude.

In verses 5-7, God patiently counsels Cain to master the sin that crouches at his door, otherwise it will rule over him. God gently and lovingly instructs fallen man here at the beginning. Knowledge of vicarious suffering for sin is reinforced. Cain, who was hoped to be *The* promised man, failed to submit himself in the things of God. Cain failed to obey God's Word. This passage captures the struggle of all humanity, the struggle with our broken and sinful nature. It also shows God's grace for us in the midst of this struggle.

When Cain grew weary of God's instruction, he became angry. *"I know not: Am I my brother's keeper?"* Here is another play on the word *knowledge.* Cain is arrogant toward God, who has patience with him. In his anger and pride, he kills his brother Abel. This is the beginning of two ancestral lines. The line of Cain becomes like Cain, sinful, arrogant and wicked, rejecting God's instruction. The line of Seth, Abel's replacement, becomes the righteous line, more about Seth later.

God is very present to Cain before his sin. While the passage does not specifically indicate that the pre-incarnate Christ is present, or that God has taken on a physical manifestation, a physical manifestation cannot be ruled out because that is how he appears in previous chapters. Regardless, it is clear that God was close and personal with Cain, counseling him like a loving father. Scripture indicates that the two had several conversations concerning his penalty for murdering his brother. God is clearly present to Cain before and after his sin. Cain's rebellious attitude would separate them. This is how God comes to all of us in our temptations and brokenness. He is loving, patient, and full of grace.

Divergent Ancestral Lines

From this point on, we have two ancestral lines. The line of Cain becomes increasingly violent which influences the world with its violence. And we also have the line of Seth, which openly professes obedience to God. Cain murdered Abel. In Genesis 4:10, the voice of Abel's blood cries to God from the ground. Abel was the first martyr, and his blood cries out for vengeance. (Hebrews 12:24, Revelation 5:9-10) All righteous blood that is spilt cries out to God. God issues a judgement in verse 11. Cain was guilty of murder, which is not simply the taking of a life, but specifically a non-judicial killing. God punishes Cain by making him an unproductive farmer and vagabond upon the earth. Cain complains to God and in his complaining, he references and recognizes the broken communion between him and God. So God *"set a mark upon Cain."* God is fair in his punishment, but the consequence of that mark would eventually become a source of pride and identity to his descendents.

Because Cain is cursed in his farming, he turns his efforts toward creating the first city. He is exiled, cut off from the rest of his family, so he begins to build his own society. He does not want to be alone, so he establishes a city. A city is a place where men dwell together. But this particular society is a godless society, built out of rebellion against God.

"Then comes the building of the first city" (vs. 17). "It is manifestly

ironic that the first great effort at this exercise of social cooperation was inaugurated by murder! What is said of clothing is also true of what we call "urban life." God did not, at the beginning, place man in a city but in a garden. The city was fallen man's idea. The first city was founded by the first murderer. Indeed, the first city was founded by the first fratricide, a fact that becomes the most ironical of archetypes."[38]

Scripture will now make a delineation between city dwellers and wilderness dwellers. St. Augustine of Hippo described it as _The city of God, and the city of Man_. Scripture shows the righteous are sojourners on earth looking to the celestial city of God. While those in rebellion are unwittingly duped into setting their hope on the reputation of men. Babel would mark the first city in rebellion after the flood, when men openly defied the Most High God.

The descendents of Cain, through his son Lemmech, become very proud. Lemmech's speech in verses 23-24 shows pride in his violence and murder. This is a mark of unrepentant and fallen man, who becomes more and more twisted in his thinking. Violence, perversion and a lack of discipline become glorified in the culture when man is not tempered by submission to God.

In verses 23-24 of chapter four Lemmech proudly boasts of killing a man.
"The statement expresses Lemmech's overweening pride and his refusal to suffer any hurt without wreaking several-fold, dire revenge. This expression of arrogance, conceit, and skillful retribution, is a clever manipulation of poetic convention by which a smaller is placed before a larger one in parallel structure for distinct emphasis. This sets the background for why God sends the flood in chapter 6-9, because "violence fills the earth."[39]

Cain desired to establish a name and society for himself, and he did. It was an ungodly society filled with polygamy, violence, revenge, pride, and purely humanistic. It only took one generation for humanity to fall from God's grace into complete debauchery and self-worship.

A Picture Of Hope For Mankind

Despite the dark and discouraging life of Cain's descendents, we are given a picture of hope at the end of chapter four. The birth of Seth was a hope and consolation for Eve. Seth means "appointed." At the beginning of chapter four, Eve put her hope in Cain. Her desire was that he would be the redeemer of mankind. We see in Eve this hope that her promised seed would grow up and defeat the curse of their sin and restore communion with God. But Cain failed and murdered Abel, leaving Eve without hope until the birth of Seth.

> "When we think of Adam's fall, there are two passive participles that should come forcefully to our minds: *lost* and *cursed*. These two words sum up the human condition without Christ.

> First, man is lost. Worse, he continues to get lost. It is a mistake to think of the fallen human-being as somehow looking for God. Indeed, the very opposite is true. When the human race fell in Adam, a kind of spiritual inertia came into play, a force that kept him going in the same direction – away from God. Of himself, man had no power of initiative to reverse the movement. This is what is meant by the Fall.

> If man was to return to God, God had to take the initiative. If God had not sought man out, he would have kept going in the same direction – away. This is very clear in the biblical story of Adam's hiding from God immediately after his disobedience. He and all his descendants would still be lying low in the bushes if God had not come after him, inquiring, 'Where are you?'

> It was not that God did not know where to find Adam. It was Adam who was lost, not God. God knew where Adam was, but Adam didn't. God's query, 'Where are you?' was in-

tended to wake lost man up to his real situation. As such, it was the first proclamation of the Gospel, the merciful word that began to reverse the direction of man's existence. Indeed, it was the first step toward the mystery of the Incarnation."[40]

CHAPTER 5

The Lineage Of Seth, The Pre-Flood Patriarchs

"And to Seth, to him also there was born a son; and he called his name Enos: then began men to call upon the name of the LORD. – Genesis 4:26

"After Seth begot Enosh, Moses wrote *'At that time he began to call upon the name of the Lord.'* Because Seth had separated himself from the house of Cain, the Sethites were called by the name of the Lord, that is, the just people of the Lord."[41] *- Ephraim The Syrian*

"The Holy Spirit came upon all the righteous men and prophets, such as Enosh, Enoch, Noah and so on, to Abraham, Isaac, and Jacob." *– Cyril of Jerusalem*[42]

"We have two lines of succession, one descending from Cain and the other from the son who was born to Adam in the order of the heir of Abel who was killed and to whom Adam gave the name Seth. He is referred to in the words 'God has given me another seed, for Abel whom Cain slew.' Thus it is that the two series of generations that are kept so distinct, the one from Seth and the other from Cain, symbolize the two cities with which I am dealing with in this work, the heavenly city in exile on earth and the earthly city, whose only search and satisfaction are for and in the joys of earth." *– St. Augustine – City of God*[43]

"Seth means 'resurrection,' and the name of his son Enosh means 'man.' The name Adam also means 'man,' but in Hebrew it can be used for any human person, either male or female; as one can see from the text: 'He created them male and female; and blessed them and called their name Adam.' This text leaves no doubt that Eve was given her proper name, whereas the common noun 'adam,' or 'human being,' applied to both Adam and Eve. It was different with the name Enosh. This means 'man,' Hebrew scholars tell us, in the sense of a man as distinguished from an woman. Thus Enosh was a 'son' of 'resurrection.'" - *St. Augustine – City of God*[44]

"The purpose of this chapter, and the source of its historical importance, is its testimony to the development of the human race from Adam to Noah, citing the godly line. It appears to be God's answer to Satan's blasphemous lie: *"Ye shall not, surely die."* Death reigned, and God's Word was fully vindicated."[45]

Ten Patriarchs / Herold's

There were ten patriarchs in the line of Adam through Seth. They are Adam, Seth, Enos, Cainan, Mahalaleel, Jared, Enoch, Methuselah, Lamech, and Noah. While Cain's line was skillful in metallurgy, Seth's line built civilizations. These men grew into prophets, priests and kings. This priestly tradition bridges time from the creation to the flood.

Adam was the first priest. His son Abel was also to be a priest, but he was murdered, so Seth succeeded him as the high priest of the family.

Seth was born in the image of Adam. He was born with the stain of original sin. "The image preserves the unity of nature and substance common to a father and son. For 'whatever the Father does, the Son does likewise.' In this very fact – that the Son does all things just as the Father does – the Father's image is reproduced in the Son, whose birth from the father is as it were an act of his will, proceeding from his mind." - *Origen*[46]

Seth lived 707 years. Some attribute his longevity to the original vigor of the first humans, or to the tree of life, or to the piety and godliness of the Sethites. Cain's line has no indication of lifespan. This reported lifespan seems hard to accept and may cause us to question if we can trust this measurement of time. But it is possible that the patriarchs had a very long lifespan. Scripture tells us that early man lived long lives until the point in time when God limited man's life, which happened after the flood.

Man was created to live in eternity. Adam and Eve were not created to die, and death did not enter the world until after they sinned. A return to our original immortality is promised through Christ, and is a restoration of our original state.

The line of Seth worshipped God publicly. They *"call upon the name of the Lord."* This is the testimony that the religious worship of the community of faith was organized for the common and public worship of God. And it is significant that they know the name Yahweh/Jehovah (Lord) before the events of Exodus 6:3."[47] This shows us that they knew God and understood how they ought to approach Him. The lesson of Cain and Abel is that God had clearly indicated to the first family how to approach Him in the right way, and that when we fail to approach God in the right way, in humility and obedience to God's Word, *"sin crouches at the door."*

"There were all links in the chain leading to the woman's seed. So to speak, they were the ten first heralds sent out to proclaim the approach of The King; the ten first shadows or adumbrations (faint image or resemblance) of the great Prophet, Priest, and King to whom the faith of the church was looking forward.

1. **Adam** we know was a prophecy of Christ, the second Adam, in more than name (I Corinthians 15:45).
2. **Abel**, the first martyr, prefigured Him dying by his brother's hand. Replaced by Seth.
3. **Seth,** the Substituted One (literally: Resurrected), was

a shadow of Him who took our room instead (Romans 5:8).

4. **Enos,** The frail one, of him who, as to his human nature, was as a *"tender plant, and a root out of a dry ground"* (Isaiah 53:2).

5. **Cainan**, Possession, of him who was the gift of God (2 Corinthians 9:15).

6. **Mahalaleel**, Praise of God, of him who was not ashamed to call us brethren, saying, I will declare thy name unto my brethren, in the midst of the church will I sing praise unto thee. (Hebrews 2:11-12).

7. **Jared**, Descent, of Him who came down from heaven (John 6:38).

8. **Enoch:** The dedicated and instructed child who walked with God, and was translated that he should not see death, of him who for his people "sanctified himself" (John 17:19), in whom were hid all the treasures of wisdom and knowledge (Colossians 2:3), who with regard to his Father could say, "I do always those things that please Him (John 8:29), and who after accomplishing his divine mission on earth was received up into glory (Acts 1:11).

9. **Methuselah:** Man of the Dart, of him whom the royal psalmist sang, *"Thine arrows are sharp in the heart of the kings enemies"* (Psalm 45:5).

10. **Lamech:** Strong Youth, of the strong one whom David saw in vision raised up for Israel's help (Psalm 89:19).

11. **Noah:** Rest, of him whose sacrifice God smelled a sweet savor of rest (Ephesians 5:2)."[48]

These ten patriarchs are followed by Shem, a.k.a. Melchizidek, King of Salem (Jerusalem) who is the eleventh in the line of these heralds. Jesus takes His priesthood from this line, becoming the twelfth herald of righteousness. He carried on this line through His priesthood. His longevity is forever.

Flavius Josephus, who was a Jewish Pharisee, historian, and military general, gives life to this line of Seth in his commentary on Genesis when he writes of a legend about Adam and Seth.

"Now Adam, who was the first man, and made out of the earth, (for our discourse must now be about him,) after Abel was slain, and Cain fled away, on account of his murder, was solicitous for posterity, and had a vehement desire of children, he being two hundred and thirty years old; after which time he lived another seven hundred, and then died. He had indeed many other children, but Seth in particular. As for the rest, it would be tedious to name them; I will therefore only endeavor to give an account of those that proceeded from Seth. Now this Seth, when he was brought up, and came to those years in which he could discern what was good, became a virtuous man; and as he was himself of an excellent character, so did he leave children behind him who imitated his virtues. All these proved to be of good dispositions. They also inhabited the same country without dissensions, and in a happy condition, without any misfortunes falling upon them, till they died. They also were the inventors of that peculiar sort of wisdom which is concerned with the heavenly bodies, and their order. And that their inventions might not be lost before they were sufficiently known, upon Adam's prediction that the world was to be destroyed at one time by the force of fire, and at another time by the violence and quantity of water, they made two pillars, the one of brick, the other of stone: they inscribed their discoveries on them both, that in case the pillar of brick should be destroyed by the flood, the pillar of stone might remain, and exhibit those discoveries to mankind; and also inform them that there was another pillar of brick erected by them. Now this remains in the land of Siriad to this day."[49]

CHAPTER 6

Chapter six begins with the statement that men began to exist in great numbers, and daughters were born to them. Some indicate that the population reached into the billions.

A Description Of The Condition Of Men

At this time, the *"Sons of God"* are those of the righteous line of Seth. These were the Ten Heralds of righteousness, those who openly worshipped God.

"Sons of God," "refers to the godly line of Seth, which intermarried with the daughters of men, the ungodly line of Cain. The result of these spiritually mixed marriages brought the judgment of God upon the primeval world. While the term 'sons of God' refers to angels in some passages (e.g., Job 1:6), this is certainly not the case here. Jesus clearly taught that angels do not "...marry nor are given in marriage (Matt. 22:30)."[50] St. John in his first epistle also states, *"Beloved, now are we the sons of God, and it doth not yet appear what we shall be: but we know that, when He shall appear, we shall be like him; for we shall see him as he is."*

This statement is pivotal, because this is the righteous line who openly worship God. But they became infatuated with the daughters of Cain, and they took multiple wives. This demonstrates how they deviated from tradition by co-mingling with the line of Cain in order to satisfy their lust. God was no longer on the throne of their hearts. They allowed him to be usurped by their own desires, and all the earth would bear the consequences.

Later, in Deuteronomy, God handed down a specific command regarding marriage. Deut. 7:3-4 *"Neither shalt thou make marriages with them; thy daughter thou shalt not give unto his son, nor his daughter shalt thou take unto thy son. For they will turn away thy son from following me, that they may serve other gods: so will the anger of the Lord be kindled against you, and destroy thee suddenly."* (Also see Genesis 26:34-35.)

Polygamy – Multiple Wives

In verse three we see the result. Verse one informs us that men became great in number. Verse two tells us that they desired the daughters of men. As a result, in verse three, God chooses to limit the lifespan of man to 120 years. In Hebrew it says that God would not *"contend"* with man, so he limited his lifespan.

There were men who continued to live long lives. Notice that when this was spoken there were several men who previously existed when the statement was made, thus we see a gradual decline in the age of men.

Nephilim (Giants)

Nephilim resulted from the union of the sons of God, with the daughters of men. Hero's? "A man of great stature. The word used is 'Nephilim'... 3. Gibbor, 'mighty man', and frequently so translated in English but rendered 'giant' in job 16:14. The word corresponds very much with the English 'hero' in meaning."[51]

"More probable is the interpretation which understands them as men of violence, roving, lawless gallants, 'who fall on others;' robbers, or tyrants."[52]

While it is true that angels are known as *"Sons of God"*, it is also true that angels are created beings of spirit, not flesh. There is no biblical record of their ability to reproduce, let alone reproduce with matter or flesh.

The passage makes sense when *"Sons of God"* are attributed to the righteous God fearing line of Seth, who began to compromise. The result was overbearing pride and vanity. Men of renown made a name for themselves. Their physical stature may have played a role in their reputation, but history also demonstrates that size is no determiner of stature. This idea does not end here, but even spans to our postmodern world where men of renown, "giants" such as Hitler, Lenin, Stalin, Napoleon, and Mao, captured corners of the world in humanistic pride.

"All that we indubitably know, from the authentic Scripture in the Hebrew and Christian traditions, is the fact that in the period before the flood there were many giants, all of whom belonged to the earthly city in human society, and they were sons of God descended from Seth who abandoned their holiness and sank down into the city of men."[53]

Verse 5 references the condition of the heart, note that this is the first time in Scripture that we see a reference to God weighing the thoughts and intents of the heart (Gen. 8:21, 14:1-3, Prov. 6:18, Matt. 15:19, Rom. 1:28-32).

St. Augustine, in the City of God said, "God's 'anger' implies no perturbation of the divine mind. It is simply the divine judgment passing sentence on sin. And when God 'thinks and then has second thoughts,' this merely means that changeable realities come into relation with His immutable reason. For God cannot 'repent,' as human beings repent, of what He has done, since in regard to everything His judgment is as fixed as His foreknowledge is clear. But it is only by the use of such human expressions that Scripture can make its many kinds of readers whom it wants to help to feel, as it were, at home. Only thus can Scripture frighten the proud and arouse the slothful, provoke inquiries and provide food for the convinced. This is possible only when Scripture gets right down to the level of the lowliest readers."[54]

Noah finds Grace with God verses 8-13. *"He was just and perfect in his generations, and Noah walked with God."* He separated himself from the wickedness of his contemporaries and followed the Lord. Verse 11 says, *"The Earth was filled with violence."* – Do we see evidence of this in our day? Again in verse 13, violence is the main reason God judges the world by destroying all flesh save for Noah and his family.

"Because the sons of Seth were going into the daughters of Cain, they turned away from their first wives whom they had previously taken. These wives, too, disdained their own continence and now, because of their husbands, quickly began to abandon their modesty, which up until that time they had preserved for their husbands' sake. It is because of this wantonness that assailed both the men and the women that Scripture says, 'All flesh corrupted its path.'"[55]

Building The Ark

Therefore God commanded Noah to build an ark made of wood from a resinous wood that resists corruption. *"Gopher wood"* is unknown today. So here we again see the use of the tree in salvation. The Garden contained trees which served as food for Adam and Eve. These trees also seemed to have certain properties which imparted knowledge or life. The Cross is a tree, and Christ Jesus was offered upon it. He became our fruit and is in the midst of the Church.

Jerome comments on the symbolism of the Ark, "We read in Genesis that the ark that Noah built was three hundred cubits long, fifty cubits wide, and thirty cubits high. Notice the mystical significance of the numbers. In the number fifty, penance is symbolized because the fiftieth psalm of King David is the prayer of his repentance. Three hundred contains the symbol of crucifixion. The letter T is the sign for three hundred, whence Ezekiel says, 'Mark THAV on the forehead of those who moan; and do not kill any marked with THAV.' No one marked with the sign of the Cross on his forehead can be struck by the devil; he is not able to efface this sign, only sin can. We have spoken of the ark, of the number fifty, of the number three hundred. Let us comment on the number thirty because the ark was thirty cubits high and finished above in one cubit. First, we repent in the number fifty; then, through penance, we arrive at the mystery of the cross; we reach the mystery of the cross through the perfect Word that is Christ. As a matter of fact, when Jesus was baptized, according to Luke, 'he was thirty years of age.' These same thirty cubits were finished off one cubit above. Fifty, and three hundred, and thirty were finished above in one cubit, that is, in one faith of God."[56]

"In the six hundredth year of Noah's life, in the second month, the seventeenth day of the month, the same day were all the fountains of the great deep broken up, and all the windows of heaven were opened. And the rain was upon the earth forty days and forty nights. In the selfsame day entered Noah, and Shem, and Ham, and Japheth, the sons of Noah, and Noah's wife, and the three wives of his sons with them, into the ark..."

The Promise Of A Covenant

The Latin word for covenant, "testamentum, berith, to cut or carve; hence a covenant, from the custom of passing between the divided pieces of the victims slain on the occasion of making such solemn compacts. My covenant is the already well-known covenant made with man. And thou shalt come into the ark, thou, thy sons, and thy wife, and thy son's wives with thee. This was the substance of the covenant agreement so far as Noah was concerned."[57]

Covenant Or Berith

"A covenant is an alliance of friendship between God and man, a divine constitution or ordinance with signs or pledges. It is instituted by God and also fulfilled by Him. God made several important covenants with his people:

- With Noah; a divine promise that there would be no other deluge.
- With Abraham, Isaac and Jacob; a promise to multiply their seed, give them the land of Canaan, and make them a blessing to the nations.
- With Israel at Sinai/Horeb, with a covenant sacrifice; renewed in the plains of Moab; with blessings and curses; a divine constitution of obedience and penalties for disobedience, in the form of tables of the covenant, inscribed with the ten words, placed in the ark of the covenant.
- With Phinehas; a constitution, establishing an everlasting priesthood in his line.
- With Joshua and Israel; an ordinance or constitutional agreement to serve Yahweh only.
- With David; a divine promise to the seed of David of an everlasting kingdom, the relation of sonship, and superintendence of the temple.
- With Jehoiada and the people; a constitutional agreement to be the people of Yahweh.
- With Hezekiah and the people; a constitutional agreement to reform the worship.
- With Josiah and the people; a constitutional agreement to obey the book of the covenant.
- With Ezra and the people; a constitutional agreement to put away foreign wives and observe the Law.
- The prophetic covenant; a divine promise through a series of prophets to establish a new constitution with new institutions and precepts."[58]

A Berith is, "A purely one-sided promise or ordinance or law which becomes a berith, not by reason of its inherent conceptual or etymological meaning, but by reason of the religious sanction added. From this it will be understood that the outstanding characteristic of a berith is its unalterableness, its certainty, its eternal validity, and not its voluntary, changeable nature. The berith as such is a 'faithful berith', something not subject to abrogation (to end or cancel something in a formal of official way). It can be broken by man, and the breach is a most serious sin, but this again is not because it is the breaking of the agreement in general; the seriousness results from the violation of the sacred ceremony by which its sanction was effected."[59]

A berith is not a testament, which would refer to a "last will." It is a covenant.

God promises to make a covenant with Noah. This promise was made to mankind through its High Priest Noah. Let that sink in. Noah is the High Priest of all creation, his family, and a tribal leader or prince of the line of Seth. Through Noah and his sons the world would be repopulated.

God would make a covenant in order to reassure mankind that he would never again destroy the earth by water. The sign of this covenant would be the rainbow. A visible sign that Almighty God does not forget His promises.

CHAPTER 7

Genesis chapter seven opens with the story of Noah's family going into the ark in preparation for the flood. In the last chapter of Genesis we are given the basic reasons God was forced to judge mankind. He looked at the thoughts and intents of the hearts of men and found only violence. Noah was the only one who pleased God, therefore He decided to save Noah from the coming judgment. He instructed Noah to build the ark, made a covenant with him and provided an overview of His plan. The final verse of chapter six tells us that Noah did all that God had commanded him to do; Noah was obedient.

We must believe that God exists, that he *"is."* Hebrews 11:6 says, *"without faith, it is impossible to please God."* Noah found grace because he believed. Of the possible billions of people who lived, only eight people survived. Only Noah, his wife, sons, and his sons' wives lived through the flood. Why? Because Noah believed that God existed, and that He is, *"a rewarder of those who diligently seek him"* - Hebrews 11:6.

God reveals himself to mankind in chapter three of Exodus as *"I am,"* the existent one. This is how we are to know God for all eternity. Noah believed this and saved himself and his family through that belief. God respects our efforts. That is why it says Noah *"found grace."* We don't know how feeble or effective were the efforts of Noah and his family to seek him and to live as righteous men. But we do know that his faith saved him. We know that Noah and his sons obeyed God and built the ark according to the instructions of the Lord. It took him approximately 100 years of labor and expense, 100 years of witnessing to everyone who saw the massive ship.

Not only did Noah's righteousness save him and his family, but his righteousness also saved the animals. God commanded Noah and his family to enter the ark. He instructed him to collect clean animals, seven of each kind male and female. Noah was also to collect unclean animals, two of each kind male and female. Finally, God told him to take in seven of each kind of male and female birds to keep their seed alive. The scripture is not entirely clear about how this happens. Were the animals inspired to approach the ark? Did Noah go out and collect them? The scripture only says *"they went in two by two."* That is all we know, and that is all we need to know. What scripture clearly shows is that all creation obeyed God's word and they were saved because if it.

Here we can learn from Noah because he did according to all that God had commanded. His works and righteousness speak to us. The scriptures clearly indicate that Noah did the tasks God had given him in complete obedience. Scripture records that Noah was six hundred years old when God flooded the earth, which means that at about five hundred years old, God gave Noah instructions to build a massive boat on dry land, far from the sea. When the ark was built, God gave specific instructions about what animals should be in the ark. As he instructed, Noah collected his family and the animals and placed them in the ark. Finally, God closed them in. We don't know if God instructed Noah in a powerful vision or in a quiet whisper. But we know that God spoke and Noah, *"did all the Lord commanded him."*

The Flood

In the beginning of Genesis God gave the waters of the earth boundaries to create dry land but in Genesis chapter seven, on the appointed day, to flood the earth God removed those bounds and water flowed from the great deep and God caused the windows of heaven to open. The waters rose 15 cubits high = 22.5 feet higher than the highest mountain. All life except what was on the ark was destroyed by the flood. The waters remained upon the earth for one hundred fifty days. The flood accomplished all that God commanded. Nothing was left alive that has breath in its nostrils. Only those in the ark survived. God's work with the flood was complete. He had preserved for himself a righteous remnant and cleansed the wickedness of the world.

CHAPTER 8

Chapter six of Genesis demonstrates why God had to bring the flood, *"and God saw that the wickedness of man was great in the earth, and that every imagination of the thoughts of his heart was only evil continually."* 6:5 – Also vs. 11 *"The earth was corrupt before God, and the earth was filled with violence."*

Upon entering the Ark in chapter seven, Noah was 600 years old. Flooding from underground springs and rain from the heavens poured for 40 days and nights; the water reached a height of 22.5 feet above the highest mountain. The waters remained upon the earth for 150 days.

Chapter eight begins, *"And God remembered Noah, and every living thing, and all the cattle that was with him in the ark: and God made a wind."* The Hebrew word for wind is *"ruach."* It's the same word used in Genesis 1:2 interpreted *"spirit"* which, *"pass(ed) over the earth, and the waters subsided."* It is the Holy Ghost, the Spirit of God, the third person of the Trinity. In the flood, God caused the waters to return to their original state during the creation process. They covered the earth. When the time came for the waters to recede, God used the same process to restore the waters back to their bounds. Even today, it is the Holy Spirit of God that holds the waters back. At the flood, they were only temporarily released at God's command.

In verse two of chapter eight, scripture says, *"The fountains also of the deep and the windows of heaven were stopped, and the rain from heaven was restrained."* Just as God caused the waters to recede in creation, we are again shown how all of nature obeys the Word of

God. Similarly, in Luke 8:24; Mark 4:39; and Matthew 8:26, Jesus calms the wind and the sea. These all demonstrate the same process. The Holy Spirit goes forth at the command of God and holds back the waters.

"*'God Remembered.'* We must not take this to mean that God had forgotten, the verb remember refers to the special attention or personal care that God gives to His own."[60] The word remember is based on the Hebrew root word *"zakar"* which means an active remembrance. If God remembers you, you have salvation. If he does not, you do not exist. Zakar means "to make present." The Greek interpretation of this word is anamnesis, which is used several times in the New Testament and means the same thing. It is an active and living memory. Remember the thief on the cross next to Jesus? He asked Jesus to remember, "anamnesis" him, when he gets to heaven. It was the same word, and it was a plea for salvation.

The ark is the vessel that saves mankind. Therefore, it is a symbol of the Cross of Christ. St. Peter explains this in 1 Peter 3:18-22, *"For Christ also hath once suffered for sins, the just for the unjust, that he might bring us to God, being put to death in the flesh, but quickened by the Spirit: By which also he went and preached unto the spirits in prison; Which sometime were disobedient, which once the long-suffering of God waited in the days of Noah, while in the ark was a preparing, wherein few, that is, eight souls were saved by water. The like figure* (antitype) *whereunto even baptism doth also now save us* (not the putting away of the filth of the flesh, but the answer of a good conscience toward God,) *by the resurrection of Jesus Christ."*

The ark is an antitype of salvation in several ways. As a type of the Mother of God, it symbolizes the womb that bore our salvation. The Orthodox Study Bible quotes an Akathist hymn which says, "The ark was a type of the Mother of God with Christ and the church in her womb. The floodwaters were a type of baptism in which we are saved."[61]

The apostles demonstrate, through their teaching, that there was much more within Scripture than the literal, obvious message. Understanding the hidden meanings of Scripture does not negate the literal or historical value, but rather reveals an underlying richness. Our Lord never wastes an opportunity to inspire. It is the Church that is the repository of the deep teachings of God. Any other source will lead us into error.

Additionally, God uses the historical event of the flood to impart a message by its connection to baptism. Just as the flood itself cleansed the world, so we are cleansed in the water of baptism. Another source put it this way:

"Noah was saved from the godless society—not so much saved from the water, as through the water from evil. For through the water of baptism the resurrected Christ, having taken his place in heaven itself, gives us a clean conscience." [62]

Finally, the flood, being the first time the world will be destroyed, prefigures the not-yet-fulfilled prophecy of the second destruction of the earth by fire. Both are a type of cleansing. Maximus of Turin teaches,

"For as Noah's ark preserved alive everyone whom it had taken in when the world was going under, so also Peter's church will bring back unhurt everyone whom it embraces when the world goes up in flames. And as a dove brought the sign of peace to Noah's ark when the flood was over, so also Christ will bring the joy of peace to Peter's church when the judgment is over, since he himself is dove and peace, as he promised when he said, 'I shall see you again and your heart will rejoice.'"[63]

"Peter's Church" in this context is the Apostolic Church, the Church catholic, or the universal Church. The reference here is a way of pointing to St. Peter as the chief apostle. Jesus said, "you are Petros, meaning rock, and upon this rock will I build my Church."

The ark then rested on the mountain range of Ararat. "Today Ararat rises about 17,000 ft. above sea level. The Ark rested on the land 74 days after the end of the 150 days while the waters subsided."[64]   The mount of Sinai, which is often referenced in Scripture, is one of the peaks in the range of Ararat. Noah sent out a raven and a dove. After about five months in the ark, they wait, perched on the top of a mountain, for the water to recede. They also wait for the command of God. *"And God spake unto Noah, saying, Go forth out of the ark..."* Noah waited until God told him to leave the ark. In vs. 16, God instructed them to leave the ark and rebuild a righteous society. Noah and his family were to *"go forth and multiply."*

The Church Fathers pondered this directive carefully. When Noah and his family entered the ark, there was no mixing of the sexes. Noah went in with his sons, and Noah's wife went in with the wives of her sons. The phrasing of the order is deliberate and demonstrates the chastity generally observed by man and animal while aboard the Ark. Furthermore, the flood was a cleansing and rebirth of the earth. This global baptism was generally restorative, it cleansed the world from the curse of Adam, so that the earth would now bring forth fruit.

"Then all creation was cleansed as if of some blemish, removing all defilement cursed in it by human wickedness. Its countenance was made resplendent; God then finally commanded the just man to disembark from the ark, freeing him from that awful prison with these words, 'Then the Lord said to Noah, 'Disembark, you and your sons, your wife and your sons wives with you, as well as all flesh, from birds to cattle; take off with you every reptile that crawls upon the earth.'' Notice God's goodness, how in everything he encourages the good man. After ordering him to disembark from the ark along with his sons, his wife, his son's wives and all the wild animals, then lest great discouragement should gradually overtake him by this further development and he become anxious at the thought that he would be on his own, dwelling alone in such a vast expanse of the earth, with no one else existing, God first said, 'Disembark from the ark, and take off everything with you,' and then added, 'Increase and multiply, and gain dominion over the earth.' See how once again this good man receives the former blessing that Adam had received before the fall. The same words were as man heard when he was created: God blessed them in the words 'Increase and multiply on the earth.' In other words, just as the former man became the beginning and root of all creatures before the deluge, so too this just man becomes a kind of leaven, beginning and root of everything after the deluge. From this point on, what is comprised in the make-up of human beings takes its beginning, and the whole of creation recovers its proper order, both the soil reawakening to productivity as well as everything else that had been created for the service of human beings."[65]

Then Noah offered right worship to the Lord for their salvation. *"Noah built an altar unto the Lord, and took of every clean beast, and of every clean fowl, and offered burnt offerings on the altar."* This is the first altar mentioned in history. It was built on a high place. Then God promises he will not again curse the ground for man's sake. Speaking distinctly of the flood, "another such world-wide catastrophe should never overtake the human race."

Verse 20 should not be overlooked. First, note the timing of the event. After the floodwaters had receded and Noah's family exited the ark, Noah's first act was to offer thanksgiving for being saved from extreme calamity. This is the first recorded ritual of sacrificial worship. It is safe to infer that this kind of worship was well-established before the flood. Note Noah's role in the process. Noah acts as the high priest, offering worship on behalf of mankind and all creatures who were saved.

The Priesthood Of The Firstborn

At this point there have been Ten Heralds (pre-flood fathers) beginning with Adam, Seth, Enosh, Cainan, Mahalalel, Jared, Enoch, Methuselah, Lemech, and Noah. Looking back to chapter five, it is worth pointing out that each man lived an astonishing length of years and had many children. Many of these children were not mentioned by name. It is only the first-born male of each generation that is listed.

There is one exception to this rule, and that is Seth. Remember that Cain was Adam's first child. Cain, who was taught by God, rejected God's instruction and murdered his righteous brother Abel. Adam had no godly child to pass on the priesthood to until Seth is mentioned. It was through Seth, who was not the first-born, that the tribal priesthood of the family of Adam would re-align. From this point on, each successive first-born would successfully bear the mantle of family or tribal priest, that is unless that first-born proved himself unfit.

The academic name for this is the law of primogeniture or the law of the first-born. This means that the firstborn son has the right of the headship of the family. This does not mean that each of the sons of a particular family did not act as priest and head of his own line, but that from a tribal understanding, the first-born would take up the mantle of chief. This mantle would designate the heir as priest, prophet, and king.

From this lineage of the Herold's we will see that Shem, who lived before the flood, would become the eleventh, which leaves open the twelfth place, to be filled by an everlasting First-born Son.

"And the Lord smelled a sweet savour; and the Lord said in his heart, I will not again curse the ground anymore for man's sake; for the imagination of man's heart is evil from his youth; neither will I smite anymore everything living, as I have done" (verse 21).

So the pleasing sacrifice of Noah, the primogeniture or high priest of the family, propitiated the wrath of Almighty God who restored the earth to its pre-curse (chapter 3) fruitfulness with a promise that the seasons would continue while the earth remains.

CHAPTER 9

Chapter nine has three distinct parts: the blessing of Noah; God's covenant with Noah; and the nakedness of Noah and the resulting curse of Cain, the son of Ham.

Chapter nine picks up where chapter eight left off. Noah has just exited the Ark and immediately gives thanks to Almighty God through sacrifice. This is pleasing to God and He subsequently responds by blessing Noah, which includes a covenant promise to all mankind.

The Blessing Of Noah

The language used in the blessing is written in a poetic form. This form is used so that man will remember what has been commanded and promised by God. It begins and ends with a similar thought reinforcing the directive with the focus of the passage being the very middle directive or statement called a *chiasim*. The main point of this blessing is the restoration of the fruitfulness of the ground to bring forth an abundance.

    a. *"Be fruitful, and multiply, and replenish the earth"* (Genesis 1:28-30)

    b. Man is given all flesh to eat, as opposed to only vegetation.

    c. Animals will now fear mankind, as opposed to enjoying harmony.

    d. The ground is restored to its primal fruitfulness; as a result of the flood it is now cleansed and will produce an abundance for mankind.

> e. Verse four says the blood shall not be eaten, because the blood contains the life of the animal. See the first council of the church in Acts 15:20 which parallels this requirement.
>
> f. Verses five and six say the requirement of death for those animals and humans who take the life of a man made in the image of God, which is the beginning of human government and judicial punishment.
>
> g. The command to be fruitful and multiply is once again repeated

God's Covenant With Noah

Because Noah is now the High Priest of all of God's creation, any covenant made between Noah and God is extended to all the nations of the earth, through the heads of every family. The sons of Noah were to *"be fruitful and multiply."* The result would be known as the table of nations; 70 nations would be formed from the posterity of Noah.

God is the conveyer/author of the covenant to Noah and his posterity. Mankind really has no duty in this relationship except to be obedient to God. God called it *"My Covenant."* This "connects it in our thoughts with that of the old covenant which, more than sixteen centuries earlier, He had established with mankind immediately after The Fall. Now that covenant was in substance an arrangement, disposition, proposal, or promise of mercy and salvation; and that has been the essential element in every covenant that God has made with man. So to speak, God's covenant is just another name for His formal conveyance to sinful man of the free gift of Christ and His salvation."[66]

While God's covenant did not change, the form of the covenant was changed with each new era of human history. There was, at times, a change upon the outward form or mode of representing the covenant – *a dispensation* or a Divine arrangement for communicating blessing. After the Flood onward, it was a promise of for-bearance when God said, *"neither shall all flesh be cut off any more by the waters of the Flood; neither shall there be any more flood to destroy the earth"* (Genesis 9:11).

"Usually the seal was with an offering of a sacrificial victim, being a public attestation of the binding character of the arrangement. 1. *The meritorious sacrifice:* The propitiatory offering of our Lord Jesus Christ, on the sole ground of which He is well pleased with and mercifully disposed towards the race of sinful men. 2. *The typical sacrifice:* The offering of Noah upon Ararat after emerging from the ark."[67]

The sign of the covenant is the rainbow, seen by mankind in the sky during or after a rainfall, and the same sign encircles the throne of God in heaven as a perpetual reminder of His covenant. This reference is found in Revelation 4:3, *"And He who was sitting was like a jasper stone and a sardius stone in appearance; and there was a rainbow around the throne, like an emerald in appearance."*

The perpetuity of the Covenant is to eternity, or everlasting, as found in verse 16, *"And the bow shall be in the cloud; and I will look upon it, that I may remember the everlasting covenant between God and every living creature of all flesh that is upon the earth."*

God finds great pleasure in demonstrating the soundness of his promises. He is not flighty that he will change his mind. He is not absent-minded that he will somehow forget to be gracious. He is gracious, loving, and kind. The sign and covenant is for man, and his peace. For that matter all of what has been given to man in the scriptures is for our understanding, that we might learn and be convinced of the character of Almighty Creator God, who created all that is seen for His good pleasure.

Three Lessons Of The Covenant

Since all prior covenants are fulfilled in the life and death of Jesus

Christ, it is important to understand God's use of covenants is to demonstrate His presence and faithfulness in dealing with mankind in general. *"For all the promises of God in him are yea, and in him Amen, unto the glory of God by us." - 2 Corinthians 1:20*

We learn three things from God's covenants. First, covenants demonstrate divine grace in dealing with men by means of a covenant or promise. This is usually something that man cannot fulfill on his own. Recognizing man's need God gives His Word as bond. Second, covenants demonstrate God's faithfulness in adhering to His promises, notwithstanding man's sinfulness and provocation. God is faithful even if fallen man is not. Third, being placed beneath a covenant of mercy, gives hope to fallen man. Men react differently to the unknown, some respond in fear and anxiety, they cower and choose passively not to act. Another may react in an aggressive manner and in pride resist God. God is ultimately interested in building faith, and he rewards those who seek him by faith.

The Nakedness Of Noah And The Resulting Curse Of Canaan.

This pivotal passage at the end of chapter nine sets up what is an important development in the future of mankind. Man's sin nature is not dead, and while the ground is renewed through the cleansing flood waters, man's penchant for sin would now continue through Noah's sons. This time, God will deal with this reality in a very different way. A way that will place checks on the growth of sin and the rate at which it is allowed to spread throughout the world.

The cursing of Canaan through the sin of Ham presents translational challenges. It is understood that the transgression of Ham, the father of Canaan, was so heinous as to merit a curse upon his son. The inferring of some sexual misconduct is prominent, but the Bible is somewhat discreet as to the exact nature of Ham's sin.

It is important that we venture forward using other biblical passages to help us translate the passage.

It goes without saying that the fallen world, before the flood, which Noah and his sons knew, had certain customs and behaviors that made an impression upon these men. The line of Cain were proud men who sought to satisfy the desires of the flesh, the implication is that their daughters were not only attractive but seductive. The result was that the sons of God, or the line Seth, became sexually enthralled with them leaving their wives and taking the daughters of Cain as concubines. This implies further that lust caused them to abandon their witness, and adopt the perverse practices of those of the fallen line of Cain. God would need to deal with this temptation in order to preserve a righteous line. It will stand that the righteous will always be tempted through lust to abandon their faith and serve the flesh.

For Noah, these customs were rejected outright for the knowledge of the Most High. This is always a conscious choice. But the devotion by each man varies. This again is evidenced in the curse itself.

A traditional understanding of the passage would cite voyeurism as the sin, indicating that Ham did nothing more than look upon his father Noah's drunken nakedness, and consequently make fun of his father's condition to his brothers. This would be an insult remembering their fathers position of High Priest of God, Tribal Chief, and head of the family. This literal interpretation is valid and supported as is by the Church Fathers. Their allegorical insight aligns the literal interpretation with the nakedness of Christ on the Cross, drunken with the figurative wine of His Passion and mocked by the Jews.

Yet other biblical clues indicate there may have been more to his actions than a simple literal translation reveals. Would this transgression, being done in poor taste, and indicating poor character, merit such a curse upon Canaan, Ham's son? It would seem, if this is the case, then the punishment would not fit the crime.

The existence of other theories of the passage throughout history makes the issue somewhat unsettled. Theories such as the Rabbinic castration theory, which proposes that Ham castrated Noah, does not hold up under examination. Another proposes paternal incest. Again, while the sexual theme carries through, it does not fully explain why Canaan would bear the curse of his father's actions. Finally, there is the theory that Ham initiated intercourse with his mother (maternal incest), whereas Canaan was the product. This type of behavior was a power move, intended to usurp authority over the head of the family. Jacob's son Rubin, who was the firstborn of Leah, and heir apparent to the family headship (primogeniture) slept with his father's concubine with the same intent and lost the family priesthood. The resulting literal translation for the crime against his father in Hebrew was called "unutterable." What was conveyed was that the original Hebrew presents a character that is unutterable indicating the sheer disgust brought about by the action itself.

The Maternal Incest Theory

Note that this portion of chapter nine takes place at a different time, after God's blessing. We notice time compression, *i.e.* verse 20, Noah planted a vineyard. Verse 21, Noah drank wine and got drunk in his house. Obviously, Noah would have to wait for the vines to produce a harvest, then, process the ripened harvest into wine. As this was the first harvest after the cleansing of the earth, Noah failed to anticipate the strength of the wine.

The establishment of what took place between Noah, Ham and his brothers is essential in understanding why the curse was placed upon Canaan, who did not exist prior to them departing the Ark. Just what type of behavior would have merited such a response. In other words, does the punishment (being cursed in perpetuity as a slave to his brothers) fit the crime?

"Of significance is the fact that this is the first occasion in Genesis when a human being pronounces a blessing or a curse; previously it was always God who blessed or cursed. Yet in cursing Canaan and blessing Shem and Japheth, Noah's words obviously carry divine authority. For the first time we meet something which is repeated later in Genesis: those within the chosen line of the *'the seed'* are divinely empowered to bless or curse others."[68]

We find further biblical support for the maternal incest theory in Leviticus 18:6-24. Under laws governing sexual conduct, the act of uncovering ones "nakedness" is described as sexual relations with that person's wife, mother, sister, etc., and is strictly forbidden. The language in this passage suggests that Ham went into his drunken father's tent and raped his mother. The resulting offspring, Canaan, was theoretically the result of this illicit action on the part of Ham. The descendants of Canaan would delve deeply into sexual sin, worshipping gods who required sexual perversion as a type of worship. They would defile their own bodies and as a result their cultures were riddled with sexually transmitted diseases.

"The Hueristic strengths of the maternal-incest interpretation are manifold: it explains (1) the gravity of Ham's sin, (2) the rationale for the cursing of Canaan rather than Ham, (3) Ham's motivation for committing his offense, (4) the repetition of 'Ham, the father of Canaan,' and (5) the sexually charged language of the passage. In addition, biblical and ancient Near Eastern analogues for Ham's crime are easy to find, and the related passages of the Pentateuch fit together more elegantly on this interpretation."[69]

The overarching message presented within verses twenty-one through twenty-seven of chapter nine, demonstrates that while the earth had been cleansed by the flood and restored to its pre-flood fruitfulness. Mankind is not free from the wickedness of original sin. Prior to the flood, sin had increased exponentially upon the earth, namely violence and wickedness (Genesis 6:5).

This occurred because the people of the earth spoke a single language, they had a single culture. The culture consisted of two components; the righteous line of Seth, who openly worshipped Almighty God and retained His knowledge, and the unrighteous line of Cain the murderer. The one component was not enough to keep the other in check. Once the righteous line decided to intermarry with the daughters of Cain, their godly influence over the culture was diminished greatly.

Through blessing and cursing Righteous Noah, speaking by the Holy Spirit, pronounced the curse of slavery upon Canaan, the son of Ham. This marks the first mention of slavery in Scripture, and is a punishment, according to St. Augustine, "deservedly imposed on sinful man." One ancient source (Chrysostom) regarded the cursing of Canaan a harsh punishment upon Ham, who did not escape the curse, but suffered as any father would by having to see his child bear this chastisement.

Shem, the youngest (disputed, some say oldest), would see the blessing of God and receive the primogeniture, the blessing of the firstborn, receiving the family priesthood, and continuing the ministry of the line of Seth. The blessing of Shem within this section is important and should not be overshadowed by the actions of Ham. Scripture uses, again, a poetic style of writing to impute both the blessing of Shem and the curse of Canaan. This style has to be understood to catch the repetition contained within and see the underlying message. Verses 25-27 begin with the curse of Canaan, the important repetition is that after each pronouncement of blessing, Canaan's curse is repeated, *"And Canaan shall be his servant."* But what cannot be missed is the repetition of the blessing of Shem in verses 26 and 27, which first states, *"Blessed be the Lord God of Shem..."* in verse 26, followed by verse 27 a pronouncement of blessing upon Japheth, *"May God enlarge Japheth...",* then the repetition of the blessing of Shem, *"And let Him (God) dwell in the habitations of Shem."* The idea here is that the blessing of Shem is that his progeny will be forever indwelt bodily by

God.[70]

The end of chapter nine provides a glimpse as to how the Almighty God will deal with sin in the post-flood era, thus keeping sin, violence, and wickedness in check. It will lead us to the tower of Babel and the division of people into different tongues and nations. It would be by division that God's grace will triumph in keeping sin in check, allowing precious time for His glorious plan to come to its fruitful conclusion. Finally, this information will compliment the bookend to Genesis, The Revelation of St. John. What is true about humanity in Genesis will be true about humanity throughout all time.

CHAPTER 10

Table Of Nations: "The Generations Of The Sons Of Noah, A Tale Of Two Cities"

The opening genealogy of chapter ten records the offspring of Noah's sons: Shem, Ham, and Japheth. These details seem dry and unimportant, but as we progress in the study of Genesis, we'll see how this information lays the foundation for how to understand the world around us and how it is divided into nations, as well as oral and written languages and dialects.

"While the surpassing importance of this wonderful chapter is religious, 'the so-called table of nations remains, according to all results of archeological exploration, an ethnographic original document of the first rank which nothing can replace. In all essential details, its trustworthiness has been strikingly vindicated by the new light from ancient monuments."[71]

According to the Mazoretic text, there are seventy sons in the Hebrew writings. When compared to the Septuagint (the Greek translation of the Old Testament, which was existent at the time of Our Lord Jesus Christ and was used by the early church), their number increases to seventy two. "The Haggadah (Jewish Passover teaching) seems to have followed the theory of the Hellenists, who regarded the ethnological table as a scientific and complete division of mankind into three races, distributed among three separate zones. This theory is expounded in the book of Jubilees; 'and at the beginning of the thirty-third jubilee they divided the earth in three parts between Shem, Ham, and Japheth, according to their inheritance' (ch. viii.)… The total number of the countries that the children of Noah divided among their descendants was 104; of islands, 99; of languages, 72; and of scripts, 16. To the share of Japheth fell 44 countries, 33 islands, 22 languages, and 5 scripts; Ham received 34 countries, 33 islands, 24 languages, and 5 scripts; Shem, 26 countries, 33 islands, 26 languages, and 6 scripts."[72]

The church fathers saw the table of nations to be extremely important for explaining how Christians understand and interact with the world around them. Your identity, how you see yourself and how you interact with others, is shaped by your worldview. The Church, through Scripture, clearly addresses how we are to understand the world around us. St. Augustine uses the imagery of two cities, the city of God and the city of man, to demonstrate that mankind lives two distinct ways in this world. One lives by and for God, the other lives apart from God.

The prophets indicate that the salvation of the Messiah will be extended to each nation in the table nations. Their evangelization was a sign of the coming of Christ. The sending out of the seventy two during the earthly ministry of our Lord was a precursor to the Apostolic evangelization that would take place after Pentecost.

God will use the lineage of Shem, the Shemites, to not only preserve this righteous line but also to set the foundation for Christ's ministry. Today, we use the term Semite to describe the Jewish people of the literal bloodline of Abraham. The Jews would be given the promised land, the Law of Moses, and the everlasting covenant with God Almighty. He would lead them, unify them, and build a nation. When they fell into sin, he would use their folly to scatter them throughout the world where the knowledge of God would be planted within each Gentile nation, a small stronghold, and use these strongholds, later called synagogues, to launch the apostolic ministry.

After the table of nations, the text addresses Noah's son Ham, who's lust for power is passed on to his lineage.

Cush Son Of Ham Begat Nimrod

Remember the sin of Ham and his father's nakedness? If it is true that Ham was after power and dominion, we will see it in his offspring. Nimrod *"was a mighty hunter before the Lord: wherefore it is said, even as Nimrod the mighty hunter before the Lord."* The name Nimrod means "Let Us Revolt." Arab traditions record ruins named after him at *Birs–Nimrod*, which is Borsippa, and at the *Nimrud of Calah*. His activities centered first in Shinar (Babylon, Modern day Iraq) and included the building of the Tower of Babel. Then he went to Assyria (founded by sons of Shem). Some believe that since the context deals with men and not animals, his prowess in hunting deals with men, and that his hunter exploits are of a moral and spiritual nature. "Mighty Hunter" is from Genesis 6:4, and his name relates to the word *marad*, meaning, "rebel." Thus he established a thoroughly autocratic, imperialistic government, back of which stands Satan in all his rage against God. He did all this before the Lord. What he did was very significant and was a matter of concern to God Himself. God certainly knows what everybody does but this made a strong impression, just as the Sons of God did in Genesis 6:2.

"Now it was Nimrod who excited them to such an affront and contempt of God. He was the grandson of Ham (not through Canaan), the son of Noah, a bold man, and of great strength of hand. He persuaded them not to ascribe unto God, as if it was through his means they were happy (he was the first dictator), but to believe that it was their own courage which procured that happiness. He also gradually changed the government into tyranny, seeing no other way of turning men from the fear of God, but to bring them into a constant dependence on his power. He also said he would be revenged on God, for he should have a mind to drown the world again; for that he would build a tower too high for the flood waters to be able to reach! And that he would avenge himself on God for destroying their forefathers!"[73]

Chapter ten, verse nine describes Nimrod as a *"giant."* This represents a theme that will carry throughout all of scripture. The term giant may describe his physical presence, but it more accurately describes his person. It indicates his personality and his desire to "make a name" for himself. Nimrod desired to make a name for himself like every tyrant does, a name that would usurp the authority of Almighty God. In contrast, Shem, who was of the righteous line and bore the name of God, as the high priest of the family, was known to give all honor and glory to God. He was called to be "the eleventh herald" by Noah in chapter nine. The sons of Ham, especially Nimrod, would seek power and fame.

In verses 10-14, we see that Babylon was the beginning of Nimrod's kingdom. Nimrod's line produced several cities along the Euphrates, found in modern day Iraq and Iran, all the way down to the Persian Gulf.

Verses 15-20 of the lineage deal with the offspring of Canaan. The sons of Canaan worshiped gods who were sexually perverse. The people were descendants of a wicked father. They inherited an awful curse. They possessed a fair domain, a beautiful land, but by usurping it from the rightful owners. There are lessons to be learned from the Canaanites. First, wicked men and nations may greatly prosper but prosperity leads to greater wickedness. The greatest prosperity cannot turn aside the punishment of sin. However, the punishment of sin did not preclude individual salvation; remember Rahab and Hiram, King of Tyre, who gave materials for the temple.

In verses 21-31 we see the lineage of Shem. Shem was blessed above his two elder brothers, receiving the family priesthood/tribal headship from Noah. As mentioned earlier, Noah was the tenth herald from Adam through Seth, a herald of righteousness, and Shem would follow as the eleventh herold. It becomes evident through Abraham that the firstborn would receive the primogeniture (birthright), but if the firstborn is not worthy, this honor is passed to a son that was worthy. In this case, it was Shem that led his brother by righteous conviction to cover his father's nakedness. Each firstborn that did not receive the family priesthood did something egregious to demonstrate they did not deserve the primogeniture. The children of Shem were 26 in number, of whom 5 were sons. Of note, Eber is the father of the Hebrews (vs. 21) in verse 25 we learn that the people were divided at the confusion of tongues.

The Table Of Nations

"The genealogy of division of Noah's family provides information on the future history of the geographical distribution of the people of the Near East. Clues are given about the settlement of the coastal areas, Northern Africa, Syria (Palestine) and Mesopotamia. All the major regions are thus represented, as well as most of the nations who will in some way interact with the Israelites, among them Egypt, Canaan, the Philistines, the Jebusites, Elam and Asshur. This suggests the political division of the "world" at the time this list was written and provides a definite indication that the roots of the Israelites are in Mesopotamia. There is no attempt, however, to link these people to racial divisions. Ancient people were more concerned with distinctions based on nationality, linguistics and ethnicity."[74]

This division of the nations clearly serves a purpose in God's plan of salvation. It's important to look back at the reason for the flood to understand why this division is a tool God will use to keep the epidemic of global sin in check. The global sin referenced in Genesis is a universal agreement, either by written or declared law or the lack of enforcement of written or declared law, that undermines all moral restraint and discipline. The evidence of moral decline is wonton violence, universal discord, hatred, confusion, and sexual immorality.

The division of the nations allows for the nations to police each other either by force or economic sanction. The rise of renegade political power was historically met with eventual resistance by neighboring nations. It also covers national acts of kindness to neighboring countries that might come to the aide of a nation in turmoil. In this way, differing cultural customs and values can be used to correct errant aggressive action or disaster with justice or generosity. Either way, division of the nations keeps any one national or political power from controlling and enveloping the world.

Two Lines

"Mankind without God is represented in the line of Cain. I say represented, because we have to assume that even the descendants of Seth, except Noah, are numbered among the ungodly at the time of the flood. These genealogies are based on natural descent to begin with, but their real nature is to show the discrimination between two types of people, those under grace and those under the curse. On these terms, then, Cain's godless line ends at the Flood. But sin is not so easily disposed of. The godly line of Seth, which leads to Noah, survives with one man's family only to divide again so that another godless race emerges in Canaan. Shem's line continues the line of Seth and leads to Terah the father of Abram. Shem is the Hebrew word for name, and the godless race seeks for its shem by its own efforts (Gen 11:4) only to be frustrated by the judgment of God. This contrasts with the godly line of Shem which shows we can achieve a name only as the objects of God's saving grace. The only renown that counts is to be known as the people of God who are called by His Name."[75]

St. Augustine, a Father and Doctor of the Church, wrote extensively of the two lines in his work "The City of God" 354-430 A.D. There he delves deeper into the biblical narrative and also captures the profound understanding among the early Church patri-archs of the nature and interpretation of Scripture. His writings on this subject are generally thought to reflect early Christian teaching and provide an inside look at the development of man after the flood. These insights illuminate what took place, and demonstrate what will inevitably take place in the end. We can know the end from the details of the beginning. It is not that the biblical text is silent concerning these things, it's that there are concepts within the text that are both assumed by the author (Moses, as dictated by The Pre-incarnate Christ), and made clear by a proper understanding of the text itself.

It must also be understood, as St. Paul points out in Romans chapter eleven, *"For if the firstfruit is holy, the lump is also holy; and if the root is holy, so are the branches. And if some of the branches are broken off, and you, being a wild olive tree, do not boast against the branches. But if you do boast, remember that you do not support the root, but the root supports you."* The Jews were holy and the nation of Israel had been prepared for the coming of Christ through the Law (Torah), and history.

CHAPTER 11

The Tower Of Babel

Despite the division outlined in chapter ten, the nations collectively disobey God's command to be fruitful and multiply and fill the earth. Instead, they organize and congregate at the city of Babel, in the land of Shinar. The most important details are that they spoke one language, led by Nimrod, they universally desired to thwart any effort by God to destroy the world again, and they desired to make a name *(Shem)* for themselves.

Making a name *(shem)* is a significant thread within Scripture. The man of God is known, not by his own reputation, but that of God's reputation. That is, he allows the Triune Name of God to rest upon him. He boasts not in himself, being humble, he boasts in God. Therefore, a reputation would magnify a person.

Their ambition demonstrates the ingenuity of man. Chapter eleven records the first time man-made brick and mortar is used in the construction of a dwelling. "The tower of Babel symbolizes man's arrogance and his rebellion against the authority of God. Not trusting God's promise never again to destroy the earth by flood, the men of Babel decide to build this tower as a sort of insurance policy against God's punishment. Its construction, therefore, is of a piece with all the earlier rebellions against God we have seen, starting in chapter 3."[76]

The intended purpose for Babel's great tower was to reach heaven. Their use of brick may also have had a two-fold purpose in that ceramic, if that is the type of brick constructed and fit together with mortar, would serve as a heat shield as well. Josephus wrote that Adam and Seth were astronomers who mapped the stars. According to his writings, it is their study of the stars that led them to conclude that the earth would be destroyed twice: once by water and once by fire. Josephus claims that Adam and Seth warned of this by first constructing a monument warning of a flood to come, then, by carving their message into a mountain that the earth would be destroyed by water and then by fire. The second message was carved into the mountain just in case the first monument was washed away. Josephus asserts that in the time of Christ, these monuments were still in existence.

The organizer was Nimrod, his name meant "Let us Revolt." He became the first dictator. Nimrod would seek to remove the knowledge of God by making a name *(shem)* for himself.

CONCLUSION

These first eleven chapters of Genesis are foundational to understanding the nature of fallen man and how God intimately loves us despite our wickedness. The understanding presented here through the apostolic teaching of the church and that of the Church Fathers, shows us God's ultimate purpose in the affairs of man in the world, his patient abiding while evil men seem to prosper, how He established the Church for our restoration, teaching us to understand the signs of the times.

In scripture, fallen mankind clearly does not change or evolve, but acts in a perceivable pattern that is evident throughout history beginning in Genesis. There will always be those who reject God and act out of a desire to satisfy the baser yearning of the flesh and emotion. Fallen man is presented as volatile in all his ways prone to perversion, violence and discord. The result is clearly catalogued in St. Paul's epistle to the Romans,

"For the wrath of God is revealed from heaven against all ungodliness and unrighteousness of men, who suppress the truth in unrighteousness, because what may be known of God is manifest in them, for God has shown it to them. For since the creation of the world His invisible attributes are clearly seen, being understood by the things that are made, even His eternal power and Godhead, so that they are without excuse, because, although they knew God, they did not glorify Him as God, nor were they thankful, but became futile in their thoughts, and their foolish hearts were darkened. Professing to be wise, they became fools, and changed the glory of God into an image made like corruptible man - and birds and four-footed animals and creeping things.

Therefore God also gave them up to uncleanness, in the lusts

of their hearts, to dishonor their bodies among themselves, who exchanged the truth of God for a lie, and worshipped and served the creature rather than the Creator, who is blessed forever. Amen."

In every age, there have been righteous men and wicked men. Many disdain the name of God and seek a name for themselves, either in the secular world or in the church. And so the last days will be as the days before the flood. Men will be boastful, proud, violent, hateful, lovers of self. They will seek to eradicate the knowledge of God and call for the unification of the world through a humanistic cause.

The first eleven chapters of Genesis provide wisdom for those who choose to perceive it. They are as important in addressing the base questions all men have about their origins, and identity, as addressing end-times theology. How is it possible for St. Paul to predict a great falling away from the Church when he wrote, *"For the time will come when they will not endure sound doctrine, but according to their own desires, because they have itching ears, they will heap up for themselves teachers; and they will turn their ears away from the truth, and be turned aside to fables"* (2 Timothy 4:3-4), without a firm understanding of these chapters.

Our heavenly Father has seen fit to lay everything before you in scripture so that you can maintain your peace. These foundational works demonstrate that God is longsuffering. He fully understands the nature of mankind and will be patient to allow all things to work according to His divine plan. He has made a way, a way that will become increasingly evident as we walk through Genesis. We will understand that He has been at the side of those who have come before us from the beginning and will not abandon us in the end.

Bibliography

Accordance Bible software, BDB, Brown Driver and Briggs Hebrew Lexicon software.

Alexander, T.D., *From Paradise to the Promised Land* (Grand Rapids: Baker Academic, 2002)

Bergsma, John Sietze, *Noah's Nakedness and the Curse of Canaan* (JBL, 124/1, 2005, 25-40)

Church, Leslie F., *Matthew Henry's Commentary In One Volume*

(Grand Rapids: Zondervan, 1961)

Douglas, J.D., *New Bible Dictionary, Third Edition* (Downers Grove: InterVarsity Press, 2001)

Goldsworthy, Graeme, *According To Plan,* (Downers Grove, Illinois Intervarsity Press, 2002)

Hertz, J.H., *The Pentateuch and Haftorahs* (London: Soncino Press, 1981)

Hindson, Edward, *The King James Study Bible* (Nashville: Thomas Nelson, 2013)

Kaiser, *Toward an Old Testament Theology, 82. See* C.A. Briggs, *Messianic Prophecy* (New York: Charles Scribner's Sons, 1886)

Kurian, George T., *Nelson's New Christian Dictionary, The Authoritative Resource On the Christian World* (Nashville: Thomas Nelson Publishers, 2001).

Louth, Andrew, *Ancient Christian Commentary on Scripture, Old Testament I Genesis* (Downers Grove: InterVarsity Press, 2001)

Pizzalato, Brian, *Adam: High Priest of Humanity* (CNA Catholic News Agency: https://www.catholicnewsagency.com/resources/sacraments/holy-orders/adam-high-priest-of-humanity)

Reardon, Patrick Henry, *Creation and the Patriarchal Histories* (Ben Lamond: Conciliar Press Ministries, 2008)

Schaff, Philip, *Nicine and Post-Nicene Fathers, Volume 5, Gregory of Nyssa: Dogmatic Treatises* (Peabody: Hendrickson Publishers, 2004)

Sheen, Fulton J., *Life of Christ* (New York: Image Books /Doubleday, 2008)

Sparks, Jack Norman, *The Orthodox Study Bible* (Nashville: Thomas Nelson, 2008)

Spence, H.D.M., *The Pulpit Bible Commentary*, (Grand Rapids, Eerdmans Publishing Co., 1961)

Von Hildebrand, Alice, *The Privilege Of Being A Woman*, (Naples Fl., Sapientia Press, 2007)

Vos, Geerhardus, *Biblical Theology Old and New Testaments*, (Edinburgh: Banner of Truth, 1996)

Singer, Isidor, *Jewish Encyclopedia, The Unedited Full-Text 1906*, (http://www.jewishencyclopedia.com/articles/11382-nations-and-langueges-the-seventy)

Walton, John, *The IVP Bible Background Commentary, Old Testament* (Downers Grove: InterVarsity Press, 2000)

Whiston, William, The Life and Works of Flavius Josephus, (New York: Holt, Rinehart and Winston Publishing, 1960)

---

[1] Kurian, George T., *Nelson's New Christian Dictionary, The Authoritative Resource On the Christian World* (Nashville: Thomas Nelson Publishers, 2001) p. 790; See Vincentian Canon.

[2] Louth, Andrew, *Ancient Christian Commentary on Scripture, Old Testament I Genesis* (Downers Grove: InterVarsity Press, 2001) p. 3; See To Moses Was Revealed The Beginning, Chrysostom.

[3] Ibid. p. 3; See Creation Known From Revelation, Basil The Great

[4] Ibid. p. 1; See 1:1 In the Beginning God Created the Heavens and Earth, Heaven and Earth Were Created Through the Word, Origen.

[5] Church, Leslie F., *Matthew Henry's Commentary In One Volume* (Grand Rapids: Zondervan, 1961) p. 1; See Verses 1-2 point 2.

[6] Louth, Andrew, *Ancient Christian Commentary on Scripture, Old Testament I Genesis* (Downers Grove: InterVarsity Press, 2001) p. 5; See 1:2a The Earth Was Without Form and Void, Creating Precedes Ordering, Ambrose.

[7] Hindson, Edward, *The King James Study Bible* (Nashville: Thomas Nelson, 2013) p. 7; See Commentary Notes on 1:3.

[8] Pentatuch: The first five books of the Old Testament; Genesis, Exodus, Leviticus, Numbers Dueteronomy. Also referred to as the Torah or Law of Moses.

[9] Louth, Andrew, *Ancient Christian Commentary on Scripture, Old Testament I Genesis* (Downers Grove: InterVarsity Press, 2001) p. 28; See Human Dignity Honored By This Deliberation, Chrysostom.

[10] Ibid. p. 28; See 1:26a Let Us Make Man, The Triune Consultation Over the Creation of Humans, Gregory of Nyssa.

[11] This topic is discussed further under the heading <u>Man is Given Work.</u>

[12] Louth, Andrew, *Ancient Christian Commentary on Scripture, Old Testament I Genesis* (Downers Grove: InterVarsity Press, 2001) p.54 ; See God Planted a Garden in Eden, Eden Represents the Church, Cyprian

[13] Ibid, p. 55; See The Tree of Life and the Tree of the Knowledge of Good and Evil, The Tree of Life Symbolizes Wisdom and Christ, Jerome.

[14] Ibid, p. 54; See God Planted a Garden in Eden, Why Christians Pray Facing East, Basil the Great.

[15] Goldsworthy, Graeme, *According To Plan,* (Downers Grove, Illinois Intervarsity Press, 2002) pg. 98.

[16] Pizzalato, Brian, *Adam: High Priest of Humanity* (CNA Catholic News Agency: https://www.catholicnewsagency.com/resources/sacraments/holy-orders/adam-high-priest-of-humanity)

[17] The Septuagint is the Greek version of the Old Testament. The name indicates seventy scholars were employed to translate the original Hebrew manuscripts. These were made for Greek speaking Jews in Egypt, and were the Scriptures the early Church used.

[18] Hindson, Edward, *The King James Study Bible, second Edition*, (Nashville, Thomas Nelson, 2013) pg. 12.

[19] Sheen, Fulton J., *Life of Christ* (New York: Image Books /Doubleday, 2008) p. 213; "In man, the body is a kind of a cage of the soul. In Christ, the Body was the Temple of Divinity. In the Garden of Eden, we know that man and woman were naked but not ashamed. This is because the glory of the soul before sin shone through the body and became a kind of a raiment. Here too in the Transfiguration, the Divinity shone through humanity."

[20] Schaff, Philip, *Nicine and Post-Nicene Fathers, Volume 5, Gregory of Nyssa: Dogmatic Treatises* (Peabody: Hendrickson Publishers, 2004) p. 467; On The Soul And The Resurrection. They indicate the very same thing that we have embodied in our own definition of it, wherein we said that the Resurrection is no other thing than *'the re-constitution of our nature in its original form...'* II Corinthians 4.

[21] Goldsworthy, Graeme, *According To Plan,* (Downers Grove, Illinois Intervarsity Press, 2002) pg. 103.

[22] Ibid. Pg. 104

[23] Spence, H.D.M., *The Pulpit Bible Commentary,* (Grand Rapids, Eerdmans Publishing Co., 1961) pg. 77.

[24] Hindson, Edward, *The King James Study Bible, second Edition*, (Nashville, Thomas Nelson, 2013) pg. 14.

[25] I John 2:15-17

[26] Hildebrand, Alice von, *The Privilege Of Being A Woman,* (Naples Fl., Sapientia Press,

2007), pgs. 19-20.

[27] Goldsworthy, Graeme, *According To Plan,* (Downers Grove, Illinois Intervarsity Press, 2002) pg. 106.

[28] Louth, Andrew, *Ancient Christian Commentary On Scripture, Old Testament I Genesis 1-11* (Downers Grove: InterVarsity Press, 2001) p. 98; See Genesis 3:20, The Mother of All Living, Eve Is Called Life, Clement of Alexandria.

[29] Hindson, Edward, *The King James Study Bible, second Edition,* (Nashville, Thomas Nelson, 2013) pg. 15.

[30] Louth, Andrew, *Ancient Christian Commentary on Scripture,* (Downers Grove, Illinois, Intervarsity Press, 2001) pg. 102

[31] Goldsworthy, Graeme, *According To Plan,* (Downers Grove, Illinois Intervarsity Press, 2002) pg. 104.

[32] Louth, Andrew, *Ancient Christian Commentary on Scripture, Genesis 1-11* (Downers Grove, InterVarsity Press, 2000) pg. 104.

[33] Spence, H.D.M., *The Pulpit Bible Commentary, Genesis Exodus,* (Grand Rapids, Eerdmans Publishing Co., 1961) pg. 77.

[34] Ibid. pg. 77.

[35] Ibid. Pg. 77.

[36] Goldsworthy, Graeme, *According To Plan,* (Downers Grove, Illinois Intervarsity Press, 2002) pg. 107.

[37] Ibid. Pg. 107.

[38] Reardon, Patrick Henry, *Creation and the Patriarchal Histories* (Ben Lamond: Conciliar Press Ministries, 2008) p. 50

[39] Hindson, Edward, *The King James Study Bible, second Edition,* (Nashville, Thomas Nelson, 2013) p. 17.

[40] Readon, Patrick Henry, *Creation and the Patriarchal Histories* (Ben Lomond: Conciliar Press Ministries) p. 43-44.

[41] Louth, Andrew, *Ancient Christian Commentary on Scripture, Genesis I-II,* (Downers Grove, InterVarsity Press, 2000) pg. 115.

[42] Ibid. Pg. 115

[43] Ibid. Pg. 115

[44] Ibid. Pg. 115

[45] Hindson, Edward, *The King James Study Bible, second Edition,* (Nashville, Thomas Nelson, 2013) pg. 18.

[46] Louth, Andrew, *Ancient Christian Commentary on Scripture, Genesis 1-11,* (Downers Grove, InterVarsity Press, 2000) pg. 117.

[47] Hindson, Edward, *The King James Study Bible, Second Edition,* (Nashville, Thomas Nelson, 2013) pg. 18.

[48] Spence, H.D.M., *The Pulpit Bible Commentary, Genesis Exodus,* (Grand Rapids, Eerdmans

Publishing Co., 1961) pg. 100.

[49] Whiston, William, The Life and Works of Flavius Josephus, (New York: Holt, Rinehart and Winston Publishing, 1960)

[50] Hindson, Edward, *The King James Study Bible* (Nashville: Thomas Nelson, 2013) p. 19; See Genesis 6:1-4.

[51] Douglas, J.D., *New Bible Dictionary, Third Edition* (Downers Grove: InterVarsity Press, 2001) p. 409.

[52] Spense, H.D.M., *The Pulpit Bible Commentary, Vol 1 Genesis Exodus* (Grand Rapids: Eerdmans Publishing, 1961) p. 103; See Genesis 6:4.

[53] Louth, Andrew, *Ancient Christian Commentary on Scripture, Genesis 1-11* (Downers Grove: InterVarsity Press, 2001) p. 125; See Genesis 6:4, The Men of Renown, The Nephilim A Race of Giants. Augustine.

[54] Louth, Andrew, *Ancient Christian Commentary on Scripture, Genesis 1-11* (Downers Grove: InterVarsity Press, 2001) p. 128; See Genesis 6:6-7, The Lord Grieved By Humanity, God's Anger Implies No Perturbation of the Divine Mind, Augustine.

[55] Ibid. p. 130 See Genesis 6:11-13, The Earth Corrupt in God's Sight, All Flesh Corrupted, Ephrem The Syrian.

[56] Louth, Andrew, *Ancient Christian Commentary on Scripture, Genesis 1-11* (Downers Grove: InterVarsity Press, 2001) p. 131; See Genesis 6:14, Instructions For Making The Ark, Mystical Meaning of the Dimensions of the Ark, , Jerome.

[57] Spence, H.D.M., *The Pulpit Bible Commentary, Genesis Exodus* (Grand Rapids: Eerdmans Publishing Co., 1961) p. 110.

[58] Accordance Bible software, BDB, Brown Driver and Briggs Hebrew Lexicon software.

[59] Vos, Geerhardus, *Biblical Theology Old and New Testaments,* (Edinburgh: Banner of Truth, 1996) p. 23.

[60] Hindson, Edward, *The King James Study Bible, Second Edition* (Nashville: Thomas Nelson, 2013), p. 22.

[61] Sparks, Jack Norman, *The Orthodox Study Bible* (Nashville: Thomas Nelson, 2008) p. 12

[62] Ibid. p. 1687

[63] Louth, Andrew, *Ancient Christian Commentary on Scripture, Genesis 1-11* (Downers Grove: InterVarsity Press, 2001) p. 148, Genesis 8:15-19, Everything Went Out of The Ark, The Ark Prefigures Deliverance Through the Church, Maximus of Turin.

[64] Hindson, Edward, *The King James Study Bible, Second Edition* (Nashville: Thomas Nelson, 2013) p. 22.

[65] Spence, H.D.M., *The Pulpit Bible Commentary, Genesis Exodus* (Grand Rapids: Eerdmans Publishing Co., 1961) p. 132.

[66] Spence, H.D.M., *The Pulpit Bible Commentary, Genesis Exodus* (Grand Rapids: Eerdmans Publishing Co., 1961) p. 145.

[67] Ibid. p. 146

[68] Alexander, T.D., *From Paradise to the Promised Land* (Grand Rapids: Baker Academic, 2002) p. 119: Noah's speeches highlight another important motif in the book of Genesis; this concerns the descendants of Canaan and Shem. Whereas Canaan's descendants are des-